Gloria's
LIFE PURPOSE

Spiritual Novel of Love and Morality

SAMEER ZAHR

ISBN
978-1-958122-00-6 (Paperback)
978-1-957378-99-2 (eBook)

TABLE OF CONTENTS

PROLOGUE

*G*loria Camino was outside the entrance to her school. She was holding on tightly to her books and handbag, and waiting for her designated driver to pick her up and take her home in one of her father's cars, just as usual.

But today did not go as expected.

A black van pulled to a stop besides Gloria. Two men dressed in black, and wearing masks, got out, grabbed her and pushed her into a van.

A few other University students also were hanging around near the school's entrance. They noticed Gloria being forced into the car, but although they ran after the vehicle as it sped away, none of them could clearly read what was on the license plate.

Gloria, a young and beautiful nineteen-year-old student at NYU (New York University), was shocked at what was happening. She now had a black cover over her head, and her hands tied behind her back, so there was no doubt she was being abducted.

Gloria started screaming for help, but to no avail: The car was moving at a great speed with her inside, and Gloria had no idea where the two black-dressed men were taking her.

A few minutes after her kidnapping, Gloria's driver arrived at the pickup spot. He was a few minutes late, and since he did not see Gloria waiting for him, so he got out of the car to asked the young people milling about f anyone had seen her.

One of the students told him that several of them had seen something horrible happen to her. The driver was incredulous at the news, and he immediately called his boss. The driver quickly told Luca Camino what had be fallen his daughter.

Luca was furious that someone had taken his daughter. He instructed Gloria's driver to get as many details as possible from the students who were witnesses, and then to return to his home to give him all the details.

Luca Camino was a very powerful man, and he was very influential in the northern Bronx region of the city. He also was a close friend of the Chief of Police, so he immediately called him and told him what happened.

In short order, a host of private detectives—quickly hired by Luca Camino—and police officers became busy trying to figure out what exactly had occurred, who had taken Gloria, the reasons for her snatching, and where the car holding her might be heading.

As for Gloria, the kidnappers drove the van for about an hour. They took Gloria to a place far away from the city. When the van came to a stop, the kidnappers roughly pulled her out of the vehicle, and led her down to a smelly, dark basement. They took off the material covering her head, and forced her to sit on a chair in the dirty room with her hands still tied behind her back.

As her eyes became adjusted to the dim light, Gloria expressed her outrage to at the tall and muscular man in front of her.

The man considered her silently for a moment. Then he told her that if she was quiet, she would be all right.

Gloria ceased her yelling.

Only two hours after Gloria's kidnapping, Luca's phone rang.

When Luca said hello, the voice on the other end said that Luca's daughter was in his custody, and that if he wanted her back, he would have to pay a ransom of two million dollars. Before abruptly hanging up, the caller said he would call again to inform Luca as to the place and the time to do the exchange.

Luca's mind began racing with fearful and intense thoughts as he nervously paced back and forth in his study, which was packed with people who looked at him in awe. Luca loved his daughter dearly, and he would do whatever it took to save her life...and get her back.

As Gloria waited to learn her fate, she desperately tried to stay calm. She began to pray, and as she did so, the strong belief that all will be okay enveloped her entire being. Her fears subsided, and she felt the hand of God protecting her. She listened to her inner voice, and despite the position she was in, she became reassured that this horrible ordeal would end soon.

It was at this time that Gloria realized that fear does not help, and needs to be replaced with faith and courage.

CHAPTER 1

An Early Awakening

Gloria was born in a tough neighborhood in the Bronx, one of New York City's five boroughs. Her father Luca Camino was a respected member of the Italian-American community, and arguably a leader among his people in that area.

From his home Luca ran a real estate organization that owned several buildings in the Bronx. The work he did was legitimate, despite many questioning the true source of his wealth.

Luca and his wife Luisa had three children together. Gloria, the youngest child, was born after her brother Marco and sister Maria. As a faithful churchgoing lady, Luisa made sure the Camino children attended both mass and Sunday school.

Gloria, Marco and Maria were brought up in luxury and an atmosphere of abundance. They all attended private schools, and a bodyguard almost always accompanied them on their outings and excursions. The crime level in their family's area of the Bronx was conspicuous and frequent, but any offenders knew to stay far away from the members of Luca Camino's family, in the fear that Luca would be quite vengeful if anything happened to anyone in his family.

Gloria grew up to be a tall brunette blessed with piercing brown eyes and ivory skin. At 5' 7" tall, she had a slender, llong andelegant neck enhance appeal olush Many of her male classmates were attracted to her, but hesitant to befriend her or ask her out of fear of her father and family.

Gloria was unarguably one of the most beautiful girls in her school, but she did not flaunt her beauty or use it to her advantage. Indeed, Gloria was quite different from other girls her age, most of whom were mainly interested in partying and 'having fun' with the boys. Instead, Gloria was shy, serious, and focused on her studies.

Gloria spent a good part of her free time reading self-development books, as well as those about the main religions in the world. She truly admired the teachings of Christ and Buddha, and all messages of love, forgiveness and mindfulness resonated well with her. She had so many questions, and she searched for answers from the material in which she immersed herself. She was a pacifist at heart, and was against wars or any other forms of violence. Her father Luca was right when he referred to her as, 'pure-hearted.'

Gloria possessed a strong love and appreciation for classical music and her piano lessons, but she had only a limited interest in sports. As a result, she exercised just enough to stay in good shape and health.

Gloria did have a few friends with whom she socialized, and most of these girls enjoyed a similar social status to her. As for the boys, there was one young man in particular, Andrea, who had his eye on Gloria.

Andrea was handsome, tall and popular. He was an athlete who played on the varsity basketball team. Many of the senior girls admired Andrea during his senior year in high school, but Andrea was mainly interested in Gloria.

He spotted Gloria when she would sometimes go with the other girls to the basketball games to cheer on their school's team. Andrea always noticed her when she was present in the crowd, and he arrogantly assumed that she had gone to the game just for him. This made him puzzled as to why she did not respond to any of his overtures, and would not ever hang out with him.

As a result, Andrea found Gloria even more intriguing...and quite a challenge.

One afternoon when Andrea ran into Gloria in the main hallway of the school between classes, he stopped her to ask her a question.

"Gloria, girl, I don't get it! Why do you keep giving me giving 'the cold shoulder?' What gives?'"

"Andrea, I am not giving you a cold shoulder. I am just not interested in developing a relationship with anyone at this time. I am focusing on my studies, and that is all, at this time in my life."'

"Gloria, I really would like us to become, uh, friends. I have no interest in the other girls and their overly flirtatious gestures and attitudes. So how about we go hang out at a coffee shop after school one day?'"

"I am sorry, Andrea, but no, thank you. However, you know who I am, and who my family is, so if you are truly interested in taking me out for coffee, and just coffee, you would need to clear it with my father first.'"

"Wow, really? I'd have to ask your *dad?* But your father and my father are on two opposite sides of the spectrum.'"

"I don't know anything about that, Andrea. But you really would need to talk to him first. If my father agrees, I will have a coffee or a lunch together with you, but that's all. I am only interested in friendship.'"

"Okay, okay, I'll see what I can do about that. I already know where you live, so I will stop by one day to see if he is there to receive me.'"

"Why don't you ask the bodyguard who picks me up after school, and ask him to tell my father you want to meet? This way you will not be embarrassed if he turns you down.'"

"Fine, I will."

Andrea walked off, unable to understand why he had to go through such a complicated process just to ask a girl out for coffee. He was a self-confident and quite good-looking young man, and he had become arrogant enough to think that he could pretty much get any girl he wanted with a mere 'snap of a finger.'

Yet he decided Gloria was worth going the 'extra mile.' Gloria was another story altogether, and represented a unique challenge for him. She was so beautiful... and yet also an enigma to him. Andrea just could not figure her out—although his ego made him believe that she liked him, in the way boys and girls often do.

As a result, Andrea swallowed his pride and his discomfort, and asked Gloria's bodyguard to check with her father, just as Gloria had suggested. They were both eighteen years old, and in their last year of high school, so it made sense that Mr. Camino would allow her to date.

Luca Camino was in his spacious study in his home, a big house known throughout the neighborhood as the 'Camino mansion,' when Gloria's bodyguard approached to tell him about Andrea's request.

It was not easy for Luca to consider allowing his beloved daughter to go out with Andrea. Luca already knew who the boy was, for Luca was 'at odds with' Andrea's father Luciano, who was jealous of Luca's dominant role in the region. Luca also was suspicious of his character. Besides, he adored his daughter Gloria and had big plans for her future, including the kind of man she should marry. So he decided he would ask to see her to discuss the matter.

That evening, Gloria came downstairs from her room to see her father in his study. She was not nervous at all about being summoned to meet with him, for the two of them had an enjoyable father-daughter relationship, one often full of humor and laughter.

After Gloria gave him a hug, Luca began their conversation with, "My dearest Gloria, why is this young man Andrea so interested in you? I know his father, and we are not on good speaking terms nowadays, as you may know. Do you like this boy?'"

"Father, I hardly know the young man! He is in my class, but we have hardly have ever talked. He is a popular kid at school though, and plays forward on the varsity basketball team. He is tall and good-looking, so many of the girls in my grade run after him. But as you very well know, I do not socialize with the boys, choosing to place my focus on my studies instead.'"

"That is admirable, Gloria!' Luca praised her. "But do you like him? Do you wish to be friends with him, if it were up to you?'"

"Father, I would be lying to you if I told you that I am not flattered by the fact that is pursuing me! In fact, the poor guy has been trying to get my attention for several months now, and he says I have been giving him 'the cold shoulder.' I do not know him well enough yet to even know if I would be interested in him! He may not be my type of guy.'"

"What *is* your type?" Luca asked curiously, arching an eyebrow.

"You know me well to guess that I am more interested in people who are mature and intellectual. For all I know, Andrea could be shallow and mainly interested in physical appearances alone. He may be trying to go out with me simply to show off to his other male friends that he got me to agree to such a thing, when none of the other boys could! But then again, Father, how would I know anything about his character? I do not judge people by how they look.'"

"I love what I am hearing, Gloria, and you know how much I love you and trust you. I think you should find out what he is like, and I would be very pleased if it does not go further than that, especially if he turns out to have a shallow character. I suggest you have coffee or lunch with him in the diner near the school. Spend a maximum of an hour together, and then tell me how you feel about him.'"

"That sounds fine, Dad, and thank you for your trust in me. I will keep you advised!'"

When Gloria saw Andrea the next day, she went up to him to tell told him they could have coffee or lunch together the next day at the nearby diner. Andrea was thrilled to hear the good news, and they agreed to meet up at noon.

Gloria also asked Andrea to keep the news of their meeting to himself. She saw no reason for it to get around the school that she had accepted Andrea's invitation.

When Gloria got home that evening, she spent the evening pondering the idea of meeting Andrea and what might come out of it. She thought, *I know I should not consider developing a deep and romantic relationship with him, as this would be contrary to my father's wishes. It truly would be best if Andrea and I could just be friends, even if I suspect that what he truly wants is a relationship with me that involves more than just friendship. Perhaps we could study together in the library some nights, or have a meal or ice cream together with some other friends of ours in the future from time to time. I might enjoy a break from my studies from time to time.*

The next day, the two classmates met at the diner as planned. They sat across from one another at a quiet table in the corner so they could talk more easily.

"Thank you, Gloria, for agreeing to see me. I also wish to thank your father for giving his permission. I was supposed to be practicing my game at this hour, but I would not miss this opportunity to be with you for anything else in the world!" he said in a voice full of emtion. "You are a very special young lady, and I am honored to be in your company."

His passionate tone unnerved Gloria just a bit.

"Please, Andrea, let us not take this meeting quite so seriously. We both are simply eager to learn more about each other, and that is why we agreed to come here and talk. You are a considered a 'hotshot' among the girls in school, and I am sure you could have anyone of them you please as a girlfriend! So I must inquire, *Why are you pursuing me; why do you think I am so special?*"

"Because you are different than the rest. You don't flirt with boys, you focus on your studies, and you are so secretive that no one at school can figure out what is on your mind! Of course, you are also very beautiful, yet you don't make a big deal out of it. It seems you are humble and shy. To me, you are unique, and I would love to get into your mind!"

"Andrea, my mind is my mine alone," Gloria objected in a firm tone of voice. "I do not share the secrets of my mind with anyone, even my close family and friends! So don't even try to go there! And as regards beauty, we are all beautiful in our own way. You understand I am not talking about outer beauty here; what really matters to me is the inner beauty of the person. What use is it if you are blessed with outer beauty but are an ugly person inside?"

"Gloria, we are too young to be so philosophical!" Andrea said with an eye-roll. "And why can't we enjoy our outer beauty while we have it, and are able? There is nothing wrong with it if two people like us become close, and choose to kiss and hug—or even make love, if we both agree to it, of course. We will always have time when we get older to worry about inner beauty."

"Gloria," Andrea pressed on, "it should be no surprise that I am attracted to you, and I believe you are attracted to me also, but maybe too shy to admit it or act on it. How about we go out one night to dinner or the movies, and we figure out what the chemistry we have between us is?"

"I hear you, Andrea, and I appreciate you have your own point of view. Unfortunately, I don't agree with you or it, and I must abide by my own truth regarding placing a value on inner beauty first. So, unfortunately it seems I am not your type of girl, and I am quite certain you will have better luck with another young woman. There are many beautiful young girls who would love to have the kind of fun you describe. Sorry, but that is not me. I suggest we remain friends, but not build any other hopes together.'"

"Okay, whatever you say. Think about it though, and let me know if you change your mind.'"

After this exchange, Gloria changed the subject, and the two talked only about their teachers and the classmates they both knew. She deliberately kept the conversation light, then thanked him for the lunch.

The two classmates left the diner at separate times.

Andrea left the diner quite disappointed that he could not persuade Gloria to be more willing to have fun with him. He felt humiliated and rejected, and he could not understand why she would turn him down! He was not used to being turned down by any of the girls at school, and he was a popular guy, and an athlete to boot!

When she got home that day, Gloria told her father about what had happened, and about the differing perspectives she and Andrea had on beauty and worth. Her father was pleased by her assessment of Andrea's character, and Gloria's decision that he was not worth her time in the future.

Luca then told Gloria to be careful, and to be very sure that she did not give Andrea an opportunity to deliberately hurt her feelings. He reminded her that revenge is a known trait in Andrea's family, which he knew about due to his dealings with Andrea's father Luciano.

Gloria reassured her father that she had a tremendous amount of inner strength, and he should not worry; she could handle whatever Andrea sent her way.

Gloria's rejection of the opportunity Andrea had offered her to go on a date with him to explore any chemistry between them hurt Andrea's ego. And, as the days passed, he began to feel so spurned and burned that he started wondering how he could enact some sort of revenge. One thing he knew for certain, though: He certainly should not try to hurt her physically; not only was he was afraid of her father Luca, but Gloria also had an intimidating bodyguard!

The only thing Andrea felt he really could do to get back at Gloria was to tease her and make her jealous. So he started flirting with other girls in front of her.

Gloria noticed Andrea's childish behavior at school, but she did not let it upset her. Indeed, it backfired, and only reconfirmed her opinion of Andrea as a shallow person!

Then Andrea started badmouthing Gloria to their friends, saying she was 'arrogant' and 'frigid.' These insults didn't bother her much, as Gloria was doing her best to remain oblivious to Andrea's 'trash talk' and baseless insults.

What Gloria truly did not appreciate was Andrea's claim later on that she was the one who had been running after him, and that he had dumped her for she was 'not his type.' This hit a nerve: Gloria detested people who lied for the sake of glorifying themselves! She also noticed that some of her friends began looking at her in a funny way that implied they were wondering if this had been the case.

Gloria decided not want to confront Andrea in order to get him to stop making his untrue remarks. *Such a confrontation would only give a further boost to his ego*, she thought. *Plus, I only have two more months before I graduate, so I should have the capacity and patience to withstand these false rumors!*

Besides, Gloria was especially thrilled about her upcoming high school graduation: She had when she was recommended by the school board to be class valedictorian, since she was the best student in her class.

However, Andrea kept up his lying and gossiping and, as day after day passed, his abundant untruths finally reached a level where Gloria could not take it anymore. She felt his actions were an infringement on her self-esteem and dignity.

At this point, Gloria felt she had to tell her father Luca about her feelings and what was going on. However, she specifically asked her father not to do anything hurtful to Andrea, but try to find someone with influence to talk to Andrea and ask him to stop his hurtful actions.

Luca smiled as he told his daughter calmly he would see what he could do. But on the inside, he was boiling, completely incensed to hear of Andrea's behavior and about how it was affecting his cherished daughter.

That same evening, Luca called upon two of his men and told them to grab Andrea after school. They did as Mr. Camino had instructed, quickly blindfolding and handcuffing Andrea before tossing him into their vehicle.

In the car, Andrea started screaming aloud, "Hey, what do you think you are doing? You don't know whom you are dealing with! I will make sure you pay a dear price for kidnapping me. Do you even know who I am?'"

"Shut up, just shut up!" the bigger of the two men growled.

"Who are you, and why are you doing this to me? What do you want from me?" Andrea demanded.

"Only you know what you have done wrong—so only you will pay the price for your loud mouth," the younger man answered.

When Andrea heard this comment about his mouth, he immediately thought that Gloria's father must have arranged this kidnapping as a punishment for having insulted and badmouthed his daughter. He started apologizing to the men and begging them not to hurt him. He also began promising to apologize to Gloria for what he had said.

After the car crossed several dirt roads, the men stopped the car at a steel scrap yard. They took a still-blindfolded Andrea out of the car, flinging him down onto the ground outside. After his body slammed into the ground, Andrea tearfully began begging again to be let go, and for the men not to kill him.

The biggest man then said in a smug way, "Relax! We are not going to kill you. We will just do a little something that will always remind you of your own worth, scumbag.'"

The two men stretched Andrea's arms out and put them down on a metal sheet. The younger of the two men picked up a baseball bat and, wielding it as a club, hit Andrea on his right wrist. Andrea screamed in pain as his wrist bones cracked and fractured. The men then punched him twice in his belly before tossing him back in the car.

As the men got in and the younger man began to drive the car, the bigger man laughed, "Make sure you enjoy the rest of the season playing basketball! But tomorrow you will go to the principal's office and tell him exactly what you did to insult Gloria. You are to make sure the whole school knows how you lied just to hurt her feelings, and how sorry you are. The principal should publish your statements in the school journal.

"You have *one week* for all this to be done. If not, we will take care of your other hand. It is your choice whether to tell your father Luciano, or to correct your mistake on your own. If you leak any information about us and what we and our car looks like, you will pay for it dearly. Do you understand?'"

"Yes, I do! Now, please take me to a hospital to fix my wrist! It is hurting me like hell.'"

After a short drive, the car stopped in front of a hospital's emergency entrance. Camino's henchmen dropped Andrea off, keeping the hood on his head so they would be unable to describe him, and unlocking his handcuffs only at the last second. Then they drove away at high speed so as not to give anyone a chance to recognize them or remember the license plate number on the vehicle.

The next day, Gloria was called to the principal's office at noon. When she entered the room, she saw Andrea inside with his hand wrapped up and hanging from a sling placed around his shoulder.

She looked surprised and asked what happened. Andrea didn't answer.

The principal spoke up and said, "Gloria, Andrea has told me he wishes to apologize for having badmouthed you, and for spreading rumors and lies about you. He says he plans to dictate a message that we will publish in the school journal that he is committed to immediately stopping such actions and lies, and that you have been honorable in all your dealing with him. From now on he plans to tell only the truth about you and what went on with the two of you.'"

Gloria looked at Andrea in surprise. "That is fine, although I deliberately kept my hurt feelings about what Andrea was saying to myself, as I did not want to create a big fuss about it in school. But…but why is your hand hanging like this, Andrea?"

"In case you did not know, two guys picked me up last night. They broke my wrist and asked me to apologize to you and the entire school about my bad manners. So here I am," Andrea said.

"Gloria, I have learned my lesson, and I am sorry for my foolish behavior. I deserved this punishment, and now I will not be playing basketball for I don't know how long. Please forgive me, and I hope I can make it up to you somehow. I will not tell my family who did it, and why. I just told my parents yesterday it was an accident from playing basketball.'"

"Well, I am sorry about your injury, and I hope you will feel better soon," Gloria said sincerely. "Am I still needed around here?'"

The principal shook his head no, and then dismissed her. Gloria went straight on to lunch.

On her way home after school that afternoon, Gloria asked her bodyguard if he knew anything about last night's incident. The man said nothing in response, so she decided to wait until she got home to find out anything further.

When Gloria reached home, she went straight into her father's office without knocking.

"Father, why did you do this to Andrea? He is just a foolish kid, and should not have had to endure such physical abuse! I don't believe in violence; you know that!'"

"Listen to me, sweet daughter. What this guy did to you was very, very wrong. You are a pure-hearted being who wishes no harm to anybody. You don't deserve to be treated like that by *anyone*. He blemished your reputation, and badmouthed you for no reason. I could have hurt him even more, but I decided to just send him a message that he needs to learn how to treat people with respect and truth.

"It is a pity that the boy's father did not teach him good manners. You can rest assured that incompetent excuse for a man will not bother you anymore, and your reputation is clean and intact again now.'"

"Father, I can manage on my own without resorting to such means of punishment. I would appreciate it if you restrain yourself from such actions again. The truth will come out to the surface always, and all will be fine! So *promise* me that in the future you will control yourself, so we can avoid any reactions of revenge.'"

"Gloria, what 'revenge' are you talking about? That boy's father would not dare to raise his finger against our family! Luciano knows better, and I can bet you his son isn't man enough to even tell his father as to the truth about what happened here. If he does, his father would punish him even more, out of respect to me!'"

"You don't think that Andrea will try to hurt me again, just to get some revenge?" Gloria worried.

"He will not try," Luca assured his daughter. "If he ever bothers you again, his punishment will be much different than this time," he threatened.

"Okay, okay, Father. Anyhow, I forgot to tell you that I have decided to accept New York University's offer, as it keeps me close to you and my mother, and is only a short drive from here.'"

"I am glad you are making that decision, Gloria. Have you decided what you will study there?'"

"No, I don't know yet. I am leaning towards humane subjects, and plan to stay from the field of science and medicine.'"

"Great. Gloria, I want you to know I am very proud of you, and I wish you all the best. And of course, I am always here for you.'"

"Thanks, Dad.'"

Gloria

The remaining weeks in school passed without any Gloria experiencing any distressing behavior or actions from Andrea. If and when their paths crossed, they simply greeted one another respectfully, then continued on.

Andrea had to keep his arm wrapped to protect his wrist for six weeks. Naturally he was unable to play basketball, and Gloria acknowledged this must have affected him deeply.

Gloria wondered, *Will Andrea continue to be respectful towards me? Or, is he merely pretending on the outside, while inwardly devising another hurtful plan that he plans to inflict upon me one day?*

The last day of school arrived, and Gloria gave the commencement speech at graduation. The faculty, visiting parents and family members, and Gloria's classmates all gave her a standing ovation when she reached its conclusion.

An excerpt of Gloria's speech appeared in the yearbook; it read:

> *Some of us will choose diiferent careers in the future. Some of us will not continue on the path of higher education. Some of us will choose to marry early, for they want to start a large family.*
>
> *We all choose diiferent paths for our own life journey, and we all experience life to become part of our destiny.*
>
> *No matter what we do in our future, please remember that we are much more than what we think we are. Let us learn how to think and how to feel, with the purpose of seeking joy and happiness for ourselves, and for others.*
>
> *Think big and visualize your dreams, knowing that with belief and determination all your dreams will be realized and fufilled.*
>
> *At the end of the day, what we study or do in life can only bear fruit if we believe that we will eventually hold in our hands that which we feed to our minds. In other words: Our thoughts become our things!*
>
> *If you think positive thoughts and feel good, you will be rewarded with positive results!*

After graduation, Gloria enjoyed a peaceful, calm summer. She did a ot of reading, and she also practiced her piano lessons on daily basis. A few times she went to the beach few times with her cousins, for they had a place in South Hampton, Long Island.

One of Gloria's older cousins, Eduardo, worked as a private detective in his father's company. He was a great admirer of Gloria's. He wished he could marry her, but he knew such a thing was not possible, as in American culture, first cousins do not marry one other.

CHAPTER 2

A Terrible Episode

I n mid-August, Gloria started at NYU, located in Manhattan. Her goal was to initially get a Bachelor of Arts degree. She chose four courses for her first semester: History of Religions, Psychology 101, English Literature and Music Appreciation.

Her father Luca arranged for a car and driver to take her to school in the morning, and to pick her up after she was finished with classes for the day. As her first semester in college commenced, Gloria soon became friends with two girls.

One of the girls was Gloria's classmate in her Psychology course, and the other took Music Appreciation. Gloria liked the two friends because they were reserved and serious about attending their classes, just like her.

Elvira and her friend XXX two admired Gloria in return, and kept asking her why she does not study to be an actress, since she was so beautiful. Gloria's answer was always the same: "I have a different calling other than acting.'"

Finally,

Elvira asked Gloria one day while they were sitting on a bench, "What is your calling then?'"

Gloria thought for a while before she said, "I don't know exactly yet! But it has to be something different and unique—something that would involve the moral values of mankind, or the empowerment of people to live a true and abundant life, or the enrichment of spiritual values…something along these lines! I want to live a life that does not emphasize an indulgence in shallow and material things'"

"Then why don't you go study the Bible and preach the gospel to the world?" Elvira responded facetiously, a teasing grin on her face.

"Who knows? I just might!" Gloria said in a powerful voice. "Don't make light of what I just said, Elvira; I am not joking here. What the world needs is to get out of the darkness in which so many live! So many focus on what is meaningless and perishable, and not on what is meaningful and long- lasting. You may be right about studying the Bible—and in fact, I have decided I will! And not only the Bible, but many other religious books as well.'"

"You do sound very serious about this," Elvira said in a more somber tone, now giving Gloria the respect she deserved. "What prompts you to pursue such interests? You live a comfortable life, and you can have anything you want, so why not just enjoy life to the fullest and have fun?'"

"I wish I knew why, but the person you describe is not the person you are looking at!" Gloria admitted with a shake of her head. "I have had this... this inner awareness within me ever since I was very young. I do not seek glory, fame, recognition and admiration. The biggest joy I get is when I am in a position to help people in need.'"

"You are so young, Gloria; what about having a boyfriend to go out with?" Elvira wondered. "I know that many admire you, but I have never send you respond to their overtures.'"

"I just don't have that...that desire within me. It crosses my mind of course, for I am not gay, but I don't know if I can trust men right now. I do know that when the right time comes, I will find the right person to share my life with. The 'fun' I am seeking out now is to increase my knowledge and learn from our great teachers about values and the meaning of life. I want to find the real reason I am here on this planet.'"

"Well, good luck, Gloria and may the Force be with you!'"

"Thanks, and that is very well said," Gloria said with a joyous smile.

The initial eight weeks of Gloria's first semester in college went very well. Gloria enjoyed her courses and continued to practice piano in her free hours. When she sat together with her parents around the dinner table in the evenings, Gloria would share with them some of what she had learned during the day. Her brother joined them on occasion—if he was not going out with his girlfriend, that is!

Gloria's brother Marco was twenty-three years old, and he worked as a director in his father's real estate companies.

As for Gloria's older sister Maria, she had married three years ago, when she was twenty-two. Maria and her husband did not live far from the Camino mansion, and they had a year-old baby boy whom Luca loved to have around all the time. So Maria and the rest of her family often joined Gloria and her parents for a well-cooked dinner in the Camino household.

Gloria got along well with both of her siblings, especially as they respected her privacy and left her alone to follow her passions in life.

It was a cold autumn day when Gloria was standing outside the school's main entrance on the sidewalk waiting to be picked up by her driver. She was few minutes early, as was usual for her.

All of a sudden—and at the time Gloria's driver usually showed—a dark van stopped near Gloria. Two men jumped out of the vehicle, grabbed Gloria, forced her inside, and drove away at a great speed.

Inside the van, the men forced a black hood over Gloria's head, and tied her hands behind her back.

Gloria was so scared, she began crying. When she asked them what they were doing and why, there was no response.

After a time, Gloria stopped asking and became silent herself.

They drove for some time; to Gloria, it seemed like an eternity. But after only an hour or so, the van stopped. One or both of the men dragged Gloria out of the car and inside a house, where she was forced down a staircase into a basement.

Once Gloria was pushed down on a seat in the basement, the men took her hood off and untied her hands. Gloria trembled visibly as she looked around. She saw a dark, dirty room with only a twin-size bed, and nothing else other than the chair on which she sat.

Meanwhile, over at NYU, the Camino's driver called his boss Luca, to ask if he had heard from his daughter, Gloria. He was wondering why she was not waiting for him in her usual spot waiting for him. When Luca told him no, the driver ended the call and continued to wait for Gloria.

A young man soon approached the vehicle and knocked on the passenger-side window. The driver opened it a crack, and the male student asked the driver if he was looking for a young woman.

When the driver said yes, and then offered a description of his charge, the man, who was also a NYU student, said that he saw the girl being taken by two men who had driven away fast in a black van.

The driver called Luca again and reported what he just heard. Luca flew to his feet in fear and immediately called his security people to inform them of what had happened. He then called his friend, the chief of the police department in the Bronx, to report the incident. The chief quickly promised to call his counterpart at the district where NYU was located in Manhattan.

Luca then called his cousin, who owned a private detective agency, to ask for his help. He was shocked that such a thing could happen to his daughter, and he kept scratching his head searching for some intuition or guidance. *Could Gloria have been kidnapped for a ransom,* he wondered?

Around this time, Luca knew he had to tell his wife the horrible news. Luisa, Gloria's mother, began crying and praying simultaneously after sinking into a chair. She then got up to light several candles of hope, then called her daughter Maria to tell her the horrible news. Maria immediately told her mother she would drive over and come sit with her to await word of Gloria's fate with her.

Two hours later, the phone rang. Luca picked up the receiver, and heard a man say in a strange-sounding and harsh voice, "Your daughter is with us. If you want to see her again, you must pay two million dollars within forty-eight hours. We will let you know where and when.'"

Then, the caller immediately hung up the phone without giving Luca a chance to talk or negotiate.

The thought crossed Luca's mind to call Andrea's father Luciano and ask for his help too. So he swallowed his pride and called up his once-fierce competitor.

Luca had not seen or talked to Luciano for more than two years now. Luciano lived in the south Bronx, and he had stayed away from bothering or competing with Luca.

"Hi, Luciano, this is Luca Camino. I am calling you because I need your help. You can make out of it whatever you like—you may call me weak or whatever— but I really do not care as this matter concerns my daughter, Gloria. She was kidnapped two hours ago. Two men grabbed her and took her away in a black van.

"I have just received a call from an unknown man asking for a ransom of two million dollars. Please try to check if any such van is in your neighborhood, and inquire discretely if anyone else knows about the kidnappers.'"

Luciano was quite surprised to hear Luciano was calling him, and he found the whole matter puzzling.

"I am sorry to hear this, Luca. Let me see what I can do, and I will call you if I find anything interesting to tell you. Gloria is a very good young lady, according to my son Andrea, who has spoke highly of her to me. Let us hope all will end well.'"

"By the way, Luciano, how is your son Andrea? What is he doing now? Is he away at college?'"

"No, no. He did not want to continue his higher education, and so he is learning a mechanical skill at a school in New Jersey. I have not seen him or heard from him in more than a month, actually, but I assume he is doing fine.'"

"Well, thank you, Luciano, and please keep me advised if you hear anything.'"

At this point in time, there were at least fifteen people moving around on phones or talking together in the Camino household.

Eduardo and his father, along with the private detectives from his father's company, kept on talking to Gloria's driver. They kept asking questions and telling him to repeat what he had been told by the student who saw the van speed away. When one of them asked if he knew the name of the student, the driver remembered that the student's first name was Brian.

After the driver described Brian's appearance, Eduardo decided to go NYU and look for the man. Eduardo adored Gloria, and he was determined to do whatever he could to find her.

Meanwhile, the police chief was also present at the Camino mansion, and he set up a double phone system that would record the next call from the villain that asked for the ransom.

As for Gloria's father, Luca kept on pacing back and forth; he was beside himself, and trying his best to stay calm. His son Marco remained by his side, and at one point he called their family doctor to request he come to the premises just in case...al

Around two a.m., when nothing further had happened, Luca finally agreed to Marco's request that he get some rest. The five members of Luca's team promised to that one of them would be awake the entire night; they would be sharing one-hour shifts to get a little rest.

Maria stayed with her mother Luisa up in her bedroom. Yet neither of the women could sleep that night.

Gloria's driver took Eduardo to NYU at eight o'clock the next morning. Once there, Eduardo and the driver met with the Dean of the Arts and Science department, briefing him on what had happened to Gloria. The Dean was shocked at the news, and he confirmed that she had no enemies in the classes she took. He also assured Eduardo that Gloria hardly enjoyed any social activities with anyone other than with Elvira and her friend.

Eduardo asked if he could meet Elvira and her friend, then explained that the driver of Gloria's car had spoken with a student named Brian, who had witnessed the van drive away. The Dean checked the roster of student names, and identified twenty-two that started with Brian. He said it would be difficult to call them all to find out what who witnessed the scene.

Eduardo insisted upon getting their full names and class schedules so that he, together with the driver and the Dean, could go see them in their classes so they might find the "right" Brian.

The trio visited class after class until the driver was able to identify a male student sitting in one of the classes as the eyewitness to Gloria's kidnapping. They waited for the class to finish before Eduardo introduced himself to the student. He asked Brian to repeat what he had seen the day before, and describe any other details that he could recall that might be important, such a the race and shape of the men, the van's color and license plate number, and so on.

Brian, a lean blond-haired fellow wearing glasses and a pair of faded jeans, thought for a moment before saying, "I remember two muscular white men in their thirties. They were dressed all in black, and probably about six feet tall. They grabbed the young lady on each of her sides and maneuvered her inside the van though its sliding door. I don't recall the model or brand of the car; it all happened so quickly."

"How about the size of the van? Was it small, medium or large?"

"It was not that large. It was one of those vans that had a row with three seats in the back."

"How about the license plate? Do you remember any numbers or letters on it, or perhaps the color of it?"

"I am sorry, but no. Oh, wait! The plate color was yellowish, and there was the shape of a map in the middle of the plate."

"Was there any blue in the plate?"

"No, I don't think so"

"Then it must be a New Jersey license plate. They are the ones with the state map inserted in the middle. Thank you for your time, Brian."

Eduardo later met with the two girls who were friends with Gloria. Both said they did not believe she was experiencing any trouble at all with anyone at the school; Gloria was a quiet and dignified young lady whom they, along with many other classmates, respected and admired.

Eduardo thanked the women for their time, then gave them his contact information should they think of anything that might be helpful.

Eduardo then instructed the driver to cross over via the tunnel to New Jersey. Eduardo wanted to meet with a friend living in the state whom he knew from his college days. The man currently worked currently as a detective in the police department.

Eduardo met up with him and explained the story of Gloria's recent abduction. He then asked his friend to please check all the smaller black vans in the state, especially those in the proximity of the New York City. His friend told him it might take him as much as twenty-four hours to arrange that. Eduardo told him that was fine, and he thanked him for his assistance in the matter.

It was mid-afternoon when Eduardo and the driver finally arrived back at the Camino mansion. Eduardo reported his findings to Luca, and asked him if he had received any call from the kidnappers.

"No, not yet. But did I hear you say that the van could be from New Jersey?"

"Yes, I did. But that is just a guess: Brian, the student who saw Gloria being taken, did not describe the plate as being from New York, and Brian also recalled some sort of map being on the plate. I believe only New Jersey has a state map in the middle of its plate. Why do you ask?"

"Well, when I talked to a former business associate, Luciano, last night, he happened to tell me that his son now lives in New Jersey. Luciano's son Andrea is the one who badmouthed Gloria in high school. So when you mentioned 'New Jersey,' a bell went off in my head! Do you think this is important?'"

"Perhaps...Do you know which town or city in New Jersey Andrea lives in?"

"No, but I will call Luciano again to see if he will tell me where his son is living is in New Jersey.'"

"Yes, please call him now. Meanwhile, I will check all the NJ technical schools close to New York City'"

Luca called Luciano again and asked him if he heard anything from his people, and Luciano said he had found out nothing at all. Then Luca casually asked him if his son goes to the same technical school that another mutual friend's son goes to in Paterson, New Jersey.

Luciano replied, "Yeah, that's the one. A lot of kids from the Bronx go there to study mechanics.'"

Luca ended the call by telling him his family was still searching for Gloria, and to let him know if he heard anything.

Luca then turned around and told Eduardo that Andrea was attending a mechanical school in Paterson. Eduardo took down Andrea's family name, and made a copy of Andrea's high school photo from the high school yearbook Gloria had in her room.

Eduardo told Luca he would go to Paterson first thing in the morning. His plan was to check out the school first, and then all the rental car companies in Paterson in case the van had been rented from one of them.

Luca nodded his approval before requesting his driver to go with Eduardo, and stay with him for as long as he was needed.

After his conversation with Luca, Eduardo called his detective friend in New Jersey, and asked him to focus his search on the Paterson area.

The mood at the Camino family home was somber and sad. The family was at a loss over what to do other than pray for a miracle. And so Gloria's mother Luisa prayed, and prayed, and prayed.

The next morning around eleven a.m., the phone rang. Luca signaled the detectives to turn the recorder on, and to switch on the calling number detector on as well. Once this was done, he answered the phone.

"Hello, this is Luca. Who is this?'"

"It is me again. Did you arrange for the money as I told you?'"

Without question iwho Luca asking for a ransom

"I am working on it. You very well know it is not that easy to ask a bank to make the amount of money that you are asking for in such a short time. And before I confirm to you that the money is available, I need proof that my daughter is alive and well. Can you put Gloria on? I would like to hear her voice.'"

"Let me check where she is. I will let you talk to her when I call you back."

The kidnapper quickly hung up, before, the detector device was able to identify the phone number and area code.

Five minutes later, the phone rang again. Luca heard the same voice on the other end of the phone.

"I will let you talk to your girl now. After that, you have thirty-six hours to come up with the ransom money. Here she is.'"

There was a fumbling sound, then a female's voice came on the line.

"Daddy, it's Gloria. I am sorry to put you through all this. I don't know where I am, but I am fine. They are treating me well, and I hope you can find a solution to get me out of here. I am being asked now to get off the phone, and I hope to see you soon.'"

"Don't worry, sweetheart! Be strong, and I will see you soon. I love you!'"

The harsh male voice sounded over the line again.

"If you want to see your girl again, the ball is in your court. I will call you tomorrow around five p.m. with details about the money transfer.'"

Then there was the sound of a click, and the phone call ended.

Luca felt much better now that he had he heard Gloria's voice and knew she was alive. He was fully aware of what a strong character she had, and he knew that she would do the very best she could under this unique kind of stress.

Then Luca turned to ask the police chief if he should pay the ransom, and whether he should arrange it with his bankers to prepare the money for her release.

The chief replied, "No. Gain some time first, and then we'll see.'"

As she sat alone, tied to a chair in a dark basement, Gloria decided to transcend her fears about her confinement by thinking positive, praying and meditating. It had truly helped to speak with her father, and so now she consciously chose to stop her crying, and to keep from feeling afraid.

Gloria told herself, I *have learned that there is a good reason for every event! This undesirable current situation is my opportunity to daydream about my vision of what my future will be. I am determined to abide by my belief that, at the end, Good will always win over Evil. No evil action such as my abduction is going to deter me from continuing my journey into the unknown, but sure-to- be serene, future. In fact, I can see light shining within me despite this darkness all around me!*

Gloria became increasingly confident she would be rescued, and soon.

Meanwhile, Eduardo was busy digging for relevant information in Paterson, NJ. He first went to the Paterson police department, and asked if they would authorize him to obtain a list of the students attending the mechanical school in town. He then proceeded with a letter of authority they provided; it enabled him to meet with the principal of the school, and ask if Andrea was one of the students there.

At the XXX school, the principal checked the records and confirmed that Andrea was one of their students. Eduardo noticed that the principal shaking his head as he confirmed Andrea's enrollment, and so he asked the principal as to the reason.

The principal responded,"I know who this kid is, and I must tell you, he is a troublemaker. I have almost kicked him out of school twice already! He hangs out with a bunch of kids like him who create havoc in class and disharmony among the students who are truly here to study and learn a skill. I gave him his last warning three days ago.'"

"Thank you for sharing this with me, sir. Would you also be so kind as to give me his home address? And tell me, where does he normally hang out with his friends outside the school?'"

The principal agreed, writing down the address where Andrea lived in a big house with eight other students about a mile away from the technical school. The man also jotted down the address of a nightclub that Andrea was likely to frequent with his close friends.

Eduardo thanked the principal for his help, and then proceeded to go to those car rental agencies in town that rented out minivans. There were two such agencies.

The first rental agency said they do rent out minivans, but didn't have a black one in their fleet. The second agency said they had one black van, which would only become available to rent early next week; it had been rented out three days ago.

When Eduardo asked if it was possible to get the name and number of the person who had rented the van, the agent at the counter replied that he was not allowed to give out the names and numbers of the customers.

Eduardo thanked him for his time, said he understood that policy, and left.

It was noon when Eduardo called Luca to update him. When Luca heard Eduardo was unable to obtain more detailed information from the car rental agency, Luca hung up in order to ask his police friends to request the rental agency's cooperation in the matter.

Only twenty minutes later, Luca called back. He asked Eduardo to go meet with Paterson's chief of police, who would be expecting him, and gave gave him the name and the address.

Eduardo agreed, then, before he hung up, told Luca that he planned to stay overnight in Paterson in order to tail Andrea.

Eduardo went straight to the chief's office. The chief greeted Eduardo with respect, ushered him in and closed the door to his office behind him. He explained that the mayor in town had instructed him to cooperate with an 'Eduardo,' and to do whatever was necessary to help resolve the case at hand.

After Eduardo quickly outlined the situation, the two men put their heads together, discussing what to do. They agreed that the first order of business was to obtain information from the rental agency about the people who rented the black van. The chief said that he also needed some evidence that would allow him to find out if there was any connection between Gloria's kidnapping and the people who had rented the van.

The chief of the police sent one of his detectives to the car rental agency to get the required information. Twenty minutes later, the detective called his boss and provided the name of the guy who rented the van, the man's address and the van's license plate number.

The chief told Eduardo he recognized the name. Emilio Verona was a known gangster who had been caught several times robbing banks and rich people's homes. The chief instructed his detective to drive by Verona's house and look for the van. He ordered the detective to be discrete, and to do nothing before he checked in with him again.

The detective and his partner drove to Emilio's address in the countryside, about twenty-five minutes away from the center of Paterson.

The two men arrived at the outskirts of an old farmhouse that clearly had been neglected for quite some time. The detective stayed several hundred feet away from the property as he looked around the premises with his binoculars.

To the right edge of the house he spied the back of a black van, and when he zoomed in, he was able to confirm the same license plate number as the one the chief had given him. He immediately called the chief and reported what he saw.

The chief told him to wait there, and he would send three police cars with six police officers to surround the property. Once the backup arrived, the detective should go in with three of the officers and check out the house in detail, as well as the surrounding areas. He was instructed to place Emilio and any other suspects under arrest, and bring them in for questioning.

Half an hour later, three police cars arrived and surrounded the house. All of the eight police officers got in 'ready' positions with their guns out in their hands. The detective used the horn speaker, and ordered the people inside the house to come out with their hands up; that the house was surrounded.

Barely a minute later, the main door opened and two men walked out. The detective ordered the men to put their hands on their heads and to walk closer to the closest police car. When they approached the car, the detective asked if there were other people still inside the house.

Emilio knew already that he it was best to cooperate with the police, so he said, "If you are looking for the kidnapped girl, she is down in the basement. She's unharmed. There is no one else in the house besides her."'

The detective sent two officers to down to the basement to look for the hostage while the two suspects were handcuffed and put in the back of one of the police cars.

Two minutes later, the officers walked out with Gloria. They told the detective in charge they had found her sitting on a chair handcuffed with her mouth taped and her feet tied together.

The detective called his boss and proudly announced, "We got the girl, Chief! She is with us, and unharmed. We also got the two kidnappers, one of whom is Emilio Verona. We are on our way to hand them over to you, Chief, for questioning and processing."'

"Well done, and see you soon."'

Eduardo was elated when the chief told him the good news. He immediately called Luca to inform him that Gloria was safe, and in police custody. She would be able to come home soon.

Upon hearing this news, Luca started jumping with joy, and the entire family started weeping happy tears.

Shortly thereafter, the detective and officers arrived at the police headquarters. The two suspects were held behind bars while Gloria and the detective went upstairs to see the chief.

As soon as Gloria entered the chief's office, she saw Eduardo. She immediately went towards him and gave him a hug while crying tears of relief.

The chief ordered Gloria a sandwich and some water while the detective went downstairs to interrogate the suspects.

In the interrogation room, the detective asked Emilio, "So tell me, who ordered you to kidnap the girl, and why did you agree to do it?"

"It was a young man whose name is Andrea. He is a student at the mechanical school. He gave us $10,000 in cash up front, and promised to give us $100,000 once the ransom was paid.'"

"Did you harm the young lady in any way?'"

"Absolutely not, although we did tape her mouth to stop her from screaming after we pushed her into the van. We also offered her some pills in the beginning to help her to calm down, but she refused to take them.

"No one touched her or got too near her after we brought her to the house, although we fed her well, and gave her plenty of water. That is the truth, and you can ask her yourself.

"Did Andrea call you after the kidnapping? Did he come to see the hostage for himself?'"

"Yes, he called me once a day to update me on matters. But no, he did not come to see her at all.'"

When the detective relayed Emilio's statements to his superior, the police chief felt there was sufficient evidence to arrest Andrea. He ordered his lieutenant to go the mechanical school with three other officers and to bring Andrea back to the station.

Thirty minutes later, several officers brought Andrea in. He was handcuffed and placed behind bars to await trial together with the other two men.

Eduardo thanked the chief for his good work, and then told Gloria he would bring her back home.

On the drive to the Bronx, Gloria called her parents. She didn't say much while her parents told her they were eagerly awaiting her arrival within the hour.

For the rest of the ride, Gloria remained silent.

CHAPTER 3

A Happy Return, A Surprise Decision

T he entire Camino family and a number of the family's close friends were standing at the front porch of the house waiting to receive Gloria when Eduardo drove up. They all cheered her when they saw her getting out of the car.

Gloria was hugged first by her parents, and then Maria and Marco. The others waited in line for their turn to embrace Gloria. All shed tears of joy, while Gloria simply smiled and said very little other than words of gratitude.

As soon as she finished hugging those there to greet her, Gloria excused herself to go upstairs to take a shower and change her clothes. Her mother wanted to accompany her, but Gloria told her she desired to be left alone for few minutes; she needed to regroup.

After she had some time to herself in her room, Gloria went downstairs to the living room to greet those who had come to see her and offer congratulations on her safe return. But Gloria looked tired, and she was, so she asked them if they could please hold back any questions they had about what had occurred until later. She then thanked them all for being there for her, but confessed she would really just like to go back to her bedroom to get some much-needed rest.

Gloria then went back upstairs after giving her dad a smile and a bit of a wink. She knew he understood!

Once the gathering at the Camino mansion dispersed, Luca went into his study to reflect on the recent events. After a few minutes, his phone rang. It was Luciano, Andrea's father.

"Luca, I just heard about what my son did to your daughter. I am so sorry. He deserves to be jailed for life for what he did. It is my fault, for he is my son, and so I must take full responsibility for his unconscionable actions! He is a disgrace to our family. If there is anything I can do in order for you to forgive me, please tell me, and I will do it. I am a man of honor. I want you to understand that.'"

"Luciano, the matter is not your fault. Many families have a 'black sheep' in their midst; that is just the way it sometimes is. You do not need my forgiveness, for justice will prevail here. I agree that Andrea should be in jail for a long while to learn his lesson. The best thing you can do is to not to let your son get out on bail, and to let the court decide his destiny.'"

"I promise you then, Luca, I will not bail him out. Neither will I appoint a team of lawyers to defend him. In fact, I hope the judge ends up giving him the most severe legal penalty possible for his actions.'"

Luca thought for a moment, then said, "In the event he is out sooner than expected, you should be make sure Andrea leaves the country to avoid any revenge from certain 'angry wolves.'"'

"I fully understand. I plan to denounce him as my child, and ensure that he leaves the country if he gets out. It is very hard for me to do that as he is my son, but my honor and dignity cannot be infringed upon, even by him.'"

"Good, then we have an understanding. Let us keep in touch, Luciano, and try to turn this horrible event into a renewal of our friendship.'"

"It will be my honor, Luca. Bye for now.'"

After Gloria had rested for a couple of hours, she came downstairs to a quiet house. She found Luisa in the kitchen preparing dinner. Mother and daughter hugged, and that's when Gloria told her mother she was okay; there was no need to worry about her. She had survived, and she was going to be just fine.

Then Gloria went to see her father; she was eager to ascertain what Luca's plans were, now that she was found safe and well.

She found her father in his study. They shared a long embrace before they broke apart and Luca said with fervor, "I am so happy to see you again, my sweet Gloria! We were really, really worried about you.

"I am so grateful for the detective work done by your cousin Eduardo, and for my friends in the police force who helped us track the van and the villains. At least you were not harmed physically during the ordeal, and now I leave it to the court to decide the destiny of these reprehensible men. How are you feeling?'"

"I must admit I am glad that ordeal was as short-lived as it was! It was really quite traumatic, but I managed to get through it working on ing., plan as soon as possible. It is also very good for me to hear that you will leave it to the courts to decide.'"

"I am glad you are so strong, Gloria. I also want you to know that Luciano, Andrea's father, called me. He has apologized for what his son did, and asked for forgiveness.'"

"Dad, none of this would have happened if you had left Andrea alone and not had his wrist broken. Can you promise me now you will not do anything revengeful to Andrea and his family in the future?'"

"Honestly, Gloria, I have not had time to think about any sort of revenge. I was only focused on your safety, and when I might be seeing you again! Daughter, what goes around comes around, and actually I am not sure I am interested in pursue the route of revenge again. Andrea will be in jail for a while—and there really is nothing I can do about that.'"

"I know, Dad! I meant, I don't want you to do something to hurt his family. Please do not even think about it!" she begged. "I am okay, and the whole thing. .it was just like a weird, surreal dream. Are you going to press charges against the kidnappers?'"

"Of course; I cannot let such a matter be left solely in the hands of the state Attorney General. I will appoint the top criminal lawyers in the state, and they will make sure Andrea stays in jail as long as he is alive. His father has already promised me he will not appoint any defense lawyers.'"

"But Dad, the laws differ from one state to the other! So you cannot impose what you want on the justice system.'"

"I am aware of that, Gloria," Luca laughed. "Besides, it is not for you to worry about these things; there is no need. Just focus on your education, and leave the rest for professionals to handle.'"

"Dad, I have been thinking hard lately, especially since I had so much uninterrupted time in which to do so!" Gloria said with a bit of a laugh. "I plan to finish this first semester at NYU, but then I may choose to continue my education elsewhere. I will let you know more once my thoughts become clear on this subject.'"

"Sweetheart, that sounds fine. For now, let us just celebrate your return, and enjoy our first dinner together in a while. Love you!'"

The next day Luca went straight to work, contacting his personal lawyer and instructing him to find the best criminal lawyers in the state of New Jersey to press charges against Andrea and the other two kidnappers. He then gathered his team of associates, including his son, and told them to stay calm, and not to seek revenge against Luciano or anyone else in Andrea's family.

He also selected two of his men to keep an eye on Gloria whenever she was left the Camino home, and instructed them to always be there to pick her up from classes at least thirty minutes early.

In the days to come, Gloria spent her evenings pretty much by herself, reading, studying, and practicing the piano after chatting with her parents during dinner. She did not go out because she had no interest in doing so. Several of her classmates invited her to parties and get-togethers, but Gloria preferred to think, pray and meditate in the quiet of her room. She had begun to recognize it was going to take her a while to fully recover from the traumatic experience she just had, so she decided to start a journal, hoping it would prove cathartic.

Her first entry was this:

> *I have heard and read about kidnappings, but I never thought such would happen to me! Yet I also know that nothing happens without a reason.*
>
> *What is the lesson for me from the abduction experience? What message is there for me to contemplate? Why would a quiet and reserved person like me get kidnapped for ransom? Was it due to greed and the hunger for money, or was it about revenge for having turned Andrea down about being my boyfriend?*
>
> *What goes pm in the head of people to behave like that??*
>
> *Was it my fault that I opened the door for Andrea and suggested we be close friends instead? Is Andrea better off in jail now, because he truly thought he would never be caught and believed he is invincible? Are most young men thoughtless or blind like he was?*

I know I will manage to put all this behind me soon. I also know that the answers to the above questions are in the questions themselves. So, I want to focus on what I am called to do in this life. I want to change the way I think and feel. I want to find the real purpose why I am here now. To find what is it that I really want to do.

I do know I have a burning desire to change how people think and feel, to teach them how to live a happy life and to abide by the Universal Truth. I will choose this new path in my life journey, and will not waste any more time doing anything else.

I pray for guidance to show me the way.

A few afternoons later, Gloria had tea with her mother while her father was busy elsewhere. After participating in the lighthearted discussion, Gloria asked her mother, "Mamma, you go to church every Sunday, and you pray at home every morning. Are you religious because it makes you feel good, or because it is how you grew up and it is now just a habit for you?'"

"What kind of a question is that, Gloria? Of course it makes me feel good to have faith! And yes, it is also a tradition that I enjoy doing.'"

"Do you read the Bible and understand its message?'"

"No, honey, I don't read the Bible all the time. But I understand the sermons our Catholic priest preaches in church, and I try to practice what he teaches.'"

"Do you have your own understanding about the teachings of Christ?'"
"Not really, honey. I am happy to hear the explanations given to the congregation by the priest, and you should know we cannot question what we are taught. Gloria, why all of a sudden are you asking me these questions? Are you no longer a believer in God after your ordeal?" Luisa asked, a stricken expression coming onto her face.

"No, quite the contrary, Mother! Of course I believe in God, but for me, the God I believe in is different than the God you were taught to believe in. For me, I know and adore God from the teachings of Christ, Mother Nature, Buddha's teachings and the Universal Truth as a whole.'"

"Gloria, why complicate your life and faith like that by pulling from so many religions? Choose one practice or faith, and abide by it; it is much easier! I know because I chose mine, and I am very comfortable with it.

I love being a good Catholic. You should try that out first, and then you can decide.'"

"I see your point, Mother, and I will try. But I have been doing a lot of reflecting lately, and I want to tell you I am thinking of leaving NYU and joining a convent somewhere in upstate New York. I want to become a nun, although I am not yet sure in what religious tradition.'"

Luisa jumped out of her chair and nearly upset her teacup when she heard this unexpected news.

"Are you out of your mind, Gloria?" she shrieked, for she had always believe that her daughter would marry and give her grandchildren. "You are smart and beautiful, and you have a great future just waiting for you! A *nun?* Is this...this *reflection* due to the incident that just happened? Did it turn you against men and relationships, because Andrea was so awful to you?'"

"Well, actually, that experience opened my mind to thinking differently. I believe I know what I want now. I want to serve humanity and teach my fellow citizens how to live a better life, one that is full of peace, joy and happiness.'"

"You need to become a *nun* to do that?" Luisa said, sounding flabbergasted still.

"What I have in mind is to continue studying different divine schools of thought and teachings at a Seminary until I get a degree in divinity. That will qualify me to be a good teacher on the subject.'"

"Goodness gracious! Can't you get your doctorate degree without being a nun?'"

"Mother, why do you, of all people, look down on a person becoming a nun? You are so religious and faithful yourself! As for me, living as a nun will help keep me focused on inner joy, so I am not distracted by the affairs of the world.'"

"Are you planning to tell your father about this? I know that this is not the kind of lifestyle he envisioned for you either.'"

"I might, but I wanted to discuss it with you first.'"

"I appreciate that confidence, Gloria, and if I were you, I would wait a while before bringing it up with him. He is still recovering from your ordeal, and I believe it might be too much for him to digest at the moment.'"

"Okay, I will hold back the news from him as long as it takes. But at least you know now what I am contemplating in terms of my future.'"

Gloria went back to her bedroom while her mother remained in the living room stunned by the conversation she just had with her youngest daughter. She began wondering if she should be the one to talk Gloria's news over with Luca first.

Meanwhile, Gloria was now realizing how it seemed it was going to be very, very difficult for her parents to understand her choice to be a nun and study the religions of the world. She pulled out her journal and began to write....

> *My family's thoughts are confined in a hard metal box, and it is seeming it is going to be almost impossible for them to think outside that box! Yet this is my life, not theirs. I was born through the union of my parents, but I am not from them. God created me, and I have my own soul.*
>
> *I feel deeply in my mind and heart that I belong to God, the Universal Power f I am being called by the divine voice within me to be the 'master of my fate and the captain of my soul,' so be it—and no one can stop me!*

There was a knock at her door; it was Luisa, who said that Luca would like to see her in his study.

Gloria went downstairs and proceeded to her father's study. Luca kissed her on both cheeks before introducing her to a man who was in the room with him. He explained slowly, while watching Gloria' face carefully, that the man was Luciano, Andrea's father.

Luciano approached Gloria, then went down on one knee before her. Sobbing, he clasped her hand with both of his, kissed it and asked her for forgiveness.

"Luciano, sir, please rise! It is all right, and it is very good to meet you, sir!'"

"What my son did to you is unforgivable, and I must apologize to you on behalf of my entire family. You are an angel, Miss Camino, and you did not deserve to be treated that way.'"

"Mr. XX, look at the positive side of this event! Because of it I have learnt how to forgive—which is a pure sign of love—and you have reestablished your friendship with my father as result. It seems there is always a silver lining!'"

"Well said, my dear," Luca said, pride for his daughter evident in his voice.

On her way back up to her room, Gloria smiled. *Good always conquers evil,* she thought once again. Indeed, she was quite happy to see the two old adversaries adopting a new paradigm based on peace and friendship.

Gloria reflected in her journal:

> *I am highly impressed with the transformation of my father's character so that he has become loving and forgiving. He has developed a greater respect for life, and less interest in violence. How amazing that my father, who is in his mid-fifties, is willing to change out his old thoughts and embrace a peaceful life. My abduction has opened his eyes and shown him a set of values in which he had no interest before!*

The court hearings on Gloria's abduction began, and once both sides presented their cases, the jury's verdict was that all three suspects were guilty on several counts.

Andrea received the most severe sentence: Thirty years in prison without parole. Emilio and his partner were each sentenced to ten years in prison.

Luciano did not attend the sentencing session, and had no plans to visit his son in prison.

Gloria felt sorry for Andrea when she heard about his sentence; she found it to be harsh, and very long. The news gave her the added motivation to educate today's young people to adopt a better value system. She knew that doing so would deter them from engaging in reprehensible behaviors that would alter the course of their lives.

Gloria finished out her first semester at NYC with high grades in all her courses. That, in her mind, ended her education at NYU. So by now, Gloria was itching to talk to her father about her future plans. As Gloria had requested, Luisa had kept the secret of her daughter's new desire to become a nun to herself.

So it was that on one quiet December afternoon, Gloria found herself sitting next to her father. The time had arrived to prepare for Christmas holidays, and father and daughter were both looking at the newly decorated Christmas tree, which they proudly worked on together. Clearly Luca was in a good mood, and Gloria seized the opportunity.

"Dad, I have something to tell you. Would you allow me few minutes of your time now?'"

"Of course, sweetheart! Go ahead; you have my full attention.'"

"Dad, I have given this a lot of thought and prayer. I would like to change my education program from a secular one, similar to what I am studying now, to a more spiritual one. I have decided to pursue a new path, for I believe I have a calling to serve young people by teaching them a better way of life.

"To achieve this, I plan drop out from NYU and join an institute in Manhattan that teaches religious studies. The Seminary provides online courses as an option. But also and essentially, in order for me to be in the right frame of mind and soul, I would like to spend a year living in a convent not far from here. It is called Sisters for Life, and is located in Suffern, NY.

"I will start my new Seminary courses right away while living in the convent. I believe I truly need to spend some time there to get rid of all the negative feelings I have arising from my abduction, and to calmly focus on my future career. I would like to have your blessings and agreement, Father.'"

Luca remained silent for a couple of minutes, then asked, "Does your mother know about this plan of yours?'"

"Yes, Dad. I told her already, but she asked me to keep it to myself until we had moved on past my abduction and you became more ready to hear it from me first.'"

"Can you not continue your higher education in religious studies without having to live as a nun the first year?'"

"Of course I can, but the choice to spend a year in a convent is to cleanse my soul and purify my mind in order to learn and hold positive thoughts only. Please do not look down on the choice! I consider it to be a very honorable way to get closer to God, who dwells within us.'"

"Will your mother and I be able to see you or visit you during this year?"" "Yes, of course! As I said, it is a short drive away from here. After the first year I can consider moving back to live with you, or find a place near the school until I finish my studies.""

At this point Luca asked Gloria to come and sit next to him at the sofa. He put his arm around her shoulders and said, "I am dumbfounded, not by the nature of your choice, but by the amazing person you have become. I admire your decision, and there is no way I can or should stop you from this honorable pursuit for your future. You clearly are highly gifted, and your awareness of your gift at such an early age is admirable. Gloria, I am so proud of you. You are full of love and hope for others. Of course I bless your choice, and I wish you the biggest joy out of what you will be doing. All costs are on me, of course, and I will pay them with pride.""

Gloria was delighted to hear her father say this, and she took his words as a sign to proceed in the new direction. She hugged her father while few tears of joy and gratitude streamed down and wet the big smile gracing her face.

She then went to tell her mother the good news. Luisa was relieved to learn about Luca's reaction and acceptance.

After discussing the news with her mother, Gloria went upstairs to sign and send out the applications she had already prepared for both the convent and the Seminary.

Gloria pored over the articles about the convent she had in mind, as these had explained the daily schedules of the nuns living there. The convent she had chosen allowed her to have a limited use of a cell phone and a laptop, and was not strict about communications with the outside world. On the contrary, the convent encouraged participation in community affairs. The convent's main pre-requisite was to join the prayer programs in the on-site chapel on a daily basis.

Gloria then lay on her bed, closed her eyes and started visualizing her life in the convent and the experience she was looking forward to. She intended to take Seminary courses online during the first year at the convent. She would then attend classes in person once she left the convent. She was thrilled that both parents were on board now, and she could not wait until she had her own independent life outside the Camino family home.

Gloria heard back from the convent in a fairly prompt manner. They asked her to come in for an interview on the twenty-fourth of December. She confirmed the appointment, and asked her mother to accompany her. Luisa said she would.

On the morning of December 24th, the driver took Gloria and her mother to the convent in Suffern. It was less than a one-hour drive from where they lived in the Bronx. They had an appointment with Sister Delores, the assistant to Mother Superior, and the person who was responsible for admissions.

They were greeted warmly and escorted to the office of Sister Delores. They all sat down in a small living area.

Sister Delores started the conversation.

"I welcome you to our convent and I would like to know the purpose of choosing us, Gloria."'

"I grew up in a Catholic home and my mother, who is with me here, is a devout Christian. We live about forty-five minutes away from here, so it would convenient for my parents to visit, and close to the family home. I finished one semester at NYU, but I have decided to quit. I believe I have a different calling, one in the spiritual realm.

"I want to help people become aware of their non-physical qualities, which have become dormant and non-existent in many situations. My intention is to dedicate one year of my life to learn more about the teachings of Christ while I also take online courses offered by an interdenominational Seminary in Manhattan.

"This is very good to know," Sister Delores said. "In case you are not familiar with our structure, the first year you will be predominantly accepted as an observer, or a Postulate as we call it. This does not qualify you to be considered a Nun. The Postulate candidate spends about two more years to become a Novice, and then could qualify to become a Nun, or Sister.

"Our essential rule is to be present for all prayer programs, which may include Bible studies and reading other relevant materials."

During your time at the convent you can study other courses online, but you cannot not leave the premises except for previously scheduled visits to family and for certain holidays. Family visits here can be coordinated within reason.

"You do not have to wear the formal habit that we nuns wear; a white shirt and a dark skirt will suffice. You may choose to wear a headscarf, and dark sweaters and coats during the winter period. High heels are not allowed—only flat shoes with a rubber sole to keep a more quiet environment.

"There will be times where you will be required to help out when we receive pregnant young women who have no other place to go to. There will be housekeeping chores as well. Topportunities

Any questions?"

"How about meal times and Sunday mass?" Gloria asked.

"We all take our meals together. There are also short breaks between programs. We all attend Sunday mass in the church adjacent to our building."

"When can I start?"

"You can come after the new year. We need a seventy-two-hour notice to make sure you have your small bedroom ready when you come. We also encourage donations to our convent if you attend; we do not have a set fee."

Luisa asked in a slightly worried tone, "Do you cut the hair of the candidates when they come?"

"We don't insist on that anymore, but we do ask that longer hair be bundled up in a bun."

Gloria then filled out one more form acknowledging and agreeing to the rules and regulations of the convent. Luisa also signed as a witness.

It was agreed that Gloria would start on the fifth of January.

There was long silence from Luisa on the drive back home. Gloria kept offering positive comments about the task at hand mainly to soften her mother's concern about her new disciplined way of life.

Once they got back to the Camino mansion, the women briefed Luca on their visit. After listening closely to the information, Luca told them he had decided to donate $12,000. Gloria was grateful for this gift, and informed him that she would not be considered a Nun from day one; she would be a Postulate, or a Candidate. She told her father that a candidate needed to spend at least three years before she could be ordained as a Nun, or Sister.

Gloria went upstairs to her room to unwind and to write down her thoughts and feelings in her journal. She wrote:

I am so thrilled, and I look forward to my move to the convent soon! I am grateful for the divine guidance that prompted me to choose this new path. I am happy my parents and the rest of the family are with me on this move.

I truly sense that some kind of a Mission is just waiting for me to activate it! I am energized by my vision of the future and the many unknown possibilities that await me. I have this great desire to help others, and I am sure I will be guided in due course to the best way I am to fufill this dream.

All I can do now is to put this dream out there with a strong desire and leave it to the Universe to show me the way when it is least expected. The Universal Law is so true: Ask and you shall receive.'

Gloria's entire family gathered at the house on Christmas Eve and enjoyed a scrumptious dinner prepared by Luisa and Gloria's older sister Maria. It was a joyous event, especially when Gloria shared her news. Everyone congratulated Gloria on her dreams for her future, and wished her well.

After dinner, the family exchanged gifts before going to church for midnight mass. Gloria gave her family books on how to broaden their spiritual horizons. There was one in particular that she gave to her brother Marco which she encouraged him to study, and not just read. It was the Napoleon Hill classic, *Think and Grow Rich.*

In turn, Marco handed Gloria her gift; she opened it to find a sexy nun's outfit.

Gloria looked at her jokester of a brother, and threw back at him, "When are you going to grow up Marco?'"

"It is a joke, my dear sister! I love your decision, and I promise I will grow up and become richer, just as the book says.'"

"Marco, this book is all about the secret to success that is built on the basics of the Universal Law of Attraction. Study it, and you will thank me one day.'"

Then the siblings hugged, and Marco thanked Gloria seriously, promising her he would indeed 'study' the book.

CHAPTER 4

The Road to Self-Discovery

On the morning of January 5th, 2004, Gloria went to the convent accompanied by both her parents. She had two suitcases: one for her clothes and towels, and the other for her books and laptop.

The Camino family was warmly welcomed, and Sister Delores took them to meet Mother Superior, Angelica. They all sat with the head of the convent for fifteen minutes. She told the Camino family that she came to the convent thirty-five years ago—and never left. It was her calling, she said.

Angelica also told them she understood why Gloria had a different calling, and she promised the candidate that the year she planned to spend with them should be fruitful and enlightening.

Luca thanked the Mother Superior and handed her a check as a donation. "That is very generous of you, Mr. Camino, and thank you from all of us here at the convent. We will make sure it is spent wisely. Now, Sister Dolores, please show Gloria and her parents her humble abode. Mr. and Mrs. Camino, I assure you that Gloria will be very happy with us in her time here."

Sister Delores walked the Caminos across the hallway to the other side of the convent towards the dormitory building, which had forty rooms. They walked up one level of stairs to Gloria's room.

It was small, just as Gloria had expected. The room consisted of a single bed, a small desk, a sink, a small closet and a chair. The bathrooms were outside, and served six additional rooms.

The Sister checked and approved the habit that Gloria would wear as a Postulate. Then she brought them to see the rest of the grounds, including the chapel, the dining area and the small playground in which the nuns sometimes played ball.

An hour later, Luca and Luisa said goodbye to Gloria. Luisa cried, hugging and kissing her daughter many times before she walked with her husband back to their car.

Luca was silent on the way back, looking outside the car window. Clearly he was in a pensive mood. After Luisa got ahold of her own emotions, she asked, "Are you okay, Luca? You seem to be...somewhere else.'"

"Yes, I am fine. I was thinking how the unexpected happens, and how the Universe functions in mysterious ways. I did not expect that Gloria, who is a great-looking young lady, would choose such a different lifestyle. You and I spoiled her, and gave her whatever her heart desired, and yet she chose a different path than what we anticipated would be her future! She is a unique and gifted individual, and I am certain she will be very successful in whatever she decides to do with her life.'"

"But are you basically happy about her move to the convent?'"

"Well, of course I will miss her daily presence, but she is an independent person with her own soul and calling. So yes, I am happy for her. I am actually quite proud of her. We all have a lot to learn from our young lady.'"

In the convent, Gloria went back upstairs to her room to unpack and set things up in her tiny space. She felt very much at peace with her decision.

She left her room at 11:15, as Sister Delores had asked her to come to the chapel at 11:30 in order to introduce her to the other residents of the convent. When Gloria walked in with Sister Delores, everyone else was already seated. They all stood up when they saw Sister Delores walk in with Gloria in her Postulate habit.

Sister Delores quietly asked the group to be seated as she brought Gloria to the front of the room. She then introduced her to the group, and asked them to come forward to greet Gloria one by one.

In the beginning, Gloria was a bit bashful. But she relaxed when the nuns came forward standing in line and introduced themselves. Each welcomed Gloria with a hug.

Gloria noticed there were six other Postulates, all of whom were dressed like her. There were five Novices, and the rest were all ordained Nuns or Sisters. Other than about ten elderly Sisters, the spiritual group was filled with younger women.

When the welcoming ceremony was over, they went over to the dining room.

Gloria sat with the other six Postulates in one section of a long table with benches on either side.

The young candidates repeated their names to Gloria to jog her memory before they briefly told her where they came from, and why they had chosen convent life.

One Postulate named Diana told her that she came to the convent about two months ago to sort out some emotional imbalances in her life, and so she was not sure she would stay for a longer period than a year. Another told Gloria she felt it was her calling to be ordained as a Nun, and to dedicate her life to serve others in need.

In turn, Gloria told them she was not sure yet about her long-term plan. For now she planned to spend about a year at the convent while also studying at the Seminary.

Right before the food was placed on the table, all bowed their heads and prayed silently. Very little conversation went on while eating, as the focus was on enjoying eating the food in silence.

After lunch, Sister Delores found Gloria and handed the new Postulate her schedule for the rest of the day and the rest of the week. Gloria read that there would be three daily prayer sessions of about forty-five minutes each, with the first one at 6:45 a.m., and before breakfast. Two hours each day were to be allocated to housekeeping chores. Lunch was at 12:00, with a free hour after lunch each day. Dinner was each day at 6:30, and there was free time after dinner, until all lights went out at 11:00 p.m.

Gloria was happy that she would enjoy about five hours of free time for herself and her reflections each day.

After few days Gloria became accustomed to the daily routine. She felt good, and appreciated the move to this new environment. It gave her a greater opportunity to focus on her inner being, and inspired her to listen more attentively to her inner voice. She did not miss any of the prayer programs, and she wrote down any new ideas she heard or read.

After one week, Gloria's mother came to see her on a pre-arranged visit. She brought Gloria's mail with her.

Among the letters there was an envelope from the Seminary. She opened it, and was ecstatic to read that she was accepted and could begin her classes online beginning January 15th.

Then Luisa told her how much they missed her back at home, and also how Luca had become a calmer person to be with. She added, "Your brother Marco is besides himself with excitement over the book you gave him to study! He goes around reciting quotes from the book, and swears by its author, Napoleon Hill. He is very grateful for your thoughtful gift, and sends you his love. He is telling everybody it is the best gift he ever received."

"I am so happy to hear that, Mother! This book can potentially change Marco's life if he follows its guidance. Now, how about Dad? You have said he is calmer and contemplative nowadays. You know him the best, so why do you think he has changed?"

"Well, your father is a very intuitive person. He's based his life and his choices on his strong intuition, which gave him a strong desire to take risks and see his decisions bear fruit. He is now slowing down on involving himself in matters of business, and slowly turning over these responsibilities to Marco. It seems that the recent events, starting with the kidnapping and followed by your eventual decision to move here, have given him a new perspective. Your positive outlook on life has had a great influence on him lately."

"I so like hearing this great family news! Also, I hope you will enjoy the book I gave you, Mom, which explains in depth the Universal Truth found in all religious teachings. Perhaps it will change or broaden your horizons as well.'"

Gloria then thanked her mother for coming to visit, and left to join the others for the mid-afternoon prayer program. When she came back to her room, she opened her laptop and completed her registration for the Seminary's online courses. She copied her father by email and asked him if he could pay for her tuition.

In her free time at the convent Gloria studied the gospels in the New Testament and focused on the words of Jesus Christ in particular. After her readings, she wrote down her understanding and her own interpretation of Christ's words or sermons.

During her first month at the convent, Gloria visited with Sister Delores twice. The first time was a scheduled evaluation session, so that the Sister could hear about Gloria's feelings and learning.

The second time, Gloria requested the meeting. The women met during the break after lunch.

Gloria said cheerfully, "Sister Delores, thank you for seeing me! I wanted to share with you what I have been experiencing lately right before I close my eyes to go to sleep.

"After I say my prayers kneeling down by my bed, I go to bed. It normally takes about ten minutes before I fall asleep. Lately, and during the last week in particular, I have heard a very quiet and angelic voice talking to me during this time. The thing is, it is in a language I don't understand. Do you have any idea what is happening to me?'"

"Gloria, this is very good news indeed! When you pray, you connect to God via the Holy Spirit. The Holy Spirit does not differentiate between languages and cultures, and what you are hearing is the voice of the Universal God.

"God is trying to tell you something that may not be clear yet, but it will become clear in due course. When this happens, you will understand. The more you focus and ask for clarity, the more you will understand its meaning. All you have to do is to keep your heart and mind open to ensure that. Your thoughts and your feelings ought to match together in harmony."

"I appreciate your explanation, Sister Delores, and I will follow your advice.'"

"Good. And I am here for you if you need any help down the road. Know that you are on the right track now!'"

Due to this conversation, Gloria felt enthusiastic about the new development in her spiritual life. She became even more eager to hear her inner voice talking to her, which began occurring not just in bed, but during the day also.

As the days passed, Gloria became quite close with Diana, the Apostolate who had told her the first week they met that she had come to the convent to sort out some 'emotional imbalance.' So eventually Diana informed Gloria that the man whom she loved and had wanted to marry had dumped her and fled the country. She confided to Gloria that she thought the breakup was her fault because she was ugly and undesirable.

WhenGloria heard this, she told her new friend, "Listen to me, Diana! You are not ugly, and you are beautiful inside and out. It is not your fault that this man dumped you. It is his loss that he could not keep you. Diana, everything happens for a good reason. Go within and seek guidance from above, and tell yourself time and time again how beautiful and good you are.

"We all go through similar episodes in life that are trying! You are not the only one. Use your time here to discover a new of life, and to forget the past. A whole new future awaits you! Get excited about that, and allow the readings and the prayers to lead you into a new direction. Focus on the now, and envision a happy future.'"

"Gloria, you are so wise and mature for your age," Diana responded with gratitude. "Thank you for offering such good advice! I will focus on my future, and enjoy the moment, just as you say. You are such a good example, so I will try to follow in your footsteps.'"

"No, Diana," Gloria replied humbly, "you should find your own path. You are a different soul, and you may have a different calling. Start by being happy and grateful for where you are, and for what you have. Feel the energy of this place, and absorb all the love you can receive from all of us here.'"

So touched was Diana by what Gloria had said that she hugged her and again thanked her for her love and words of wisdom.

Gloria stated to believe that she might have a gift for communicating with people; it was yet another sign on her road of self-discovery. She started visualizing herself helping many others down the road, and this opportunity opened up for Gloria when Diana shared her joy and enthusiasm over her encounter with Gloria with the other Postulates. One by one, each approached Gloria and asked if they could talk about their situation and perspective on life and faith with her. Gloria accepted these overtures and gave each the advice she was guided to give.

They all appreciated her helpful advice and insight, as well as her full and sincere compassion.

Word got out regarding Gloria and her ability to give incredibly helpful advice; the news spread fast. The Novices asked for her attention next, and

Gloria was pleased to listen to their stories and give them advice if they asked for it.

Before the end of Gloria's second month at the convent, the news about Gloria's gift of counseling reached the older nuns, and even the ear of Mother Superior, who asked to see her.

Sister Delores accompanied Gloria to see Mother Superior after lunch one day.

"Gloria, I am happy to hear from Sister Delores and others that you have become a good listener to many of the beginners at the convent. Do you enjoy this work?"

"Mother Superior, it is not a matter of enjoyment, as I do not plan these conversations in advance. My new friends approach me, and I listen to them and then consult with my inner voice on how to best respond," Gloria answered confidently.

"Yes, Sister Delores tells me that you hear voices of angels talking to you when you go to sleep. Is that still happening?'"

"Yes, and that voice is becoming clearer and clearer with time. In fact, when I am asked a question by any of the younger nuns in the convent, I am not sure if it is me who answers them back. I connect with a voice guiding me from within!'"

"Gloria, God may have given you the gift of transmuting His messages through you. Be aware of that gift, and be grateful that you have been chosen to have it. Write down what you hear and record what you say. It may take you a while longer to fully understand all that is conveyed, but be aware that yours is a unique gift, and you should cherish it.'"

The meeting ended with a big smile gracing the face of Mother Superior, who told Gloria to focus on a continued awareness of her gift.

Back in her room, Gloria reflected on her conversation with Mother Superior. She recalled that Mother Superior had never used the term 'medium,' and she liked that, for she did not want to be labeled as such.

She also remembered reading about Christ having to cast out spirited demons from people, and she did not want there to be any confusion that she was perhaps hearing from spirits or demons. Gloria absolutely knew she was only hearing the voice of God through the Holy Spirit that she believed abided in her.

The end of Gloria's first semester at the Seminary was approaching, and Gloria studied hard to prepare for the upcoming online exams. Among a host of other things she learned, she was astounded to discover it was estimated that there are 4,200 religious faiths in the world! These included all sects or different schools of thought that were offshoots from the major world religions: Judaism, Buddhism, Hinduism, Christianity, Islam and Taoism. Not all of the religions were monolithic, which referred to believing in one God. Some were mere philosophies of life, and others were polytheistic, referring to the worship or belief in multiple gods. However, almost all these religions shared a common objective: to teach man how to live a better life.

Gloria immediately reached for her journal and began to write:

How can I be useful while there are so many schools of thought—4,200, according to what I just discovered—competing with one another already? And, why are there so many religions and beliefs? There has to be a way to unify or simplify all the teachings into one common method of awareness so that people can learn about who God is.

The term 'religion' turns of many young people, and so they steer away from belief and supporting a particular tradition. Perhaps there is a common denominator to extract as a substitute to the word 'religion'? It would be great f I could come up with a term that would represent the essence of all these religions and bring people closer to God through a non-religious approach.

After four months at the convent, Gloria was quite popular in her new community. Everyone admired her deep insights and her aspiration to do good deeds through helping others, and the young in particular. All staying at the convent enjoyed their conversations with Gloria. The senior Sisters found Gloria to be very bright and intuitive, and were confident that she would be a unique messenger of Christ in the world.

Gloria managed to visit her parents three times during her first semester, including on her nineteenth birthday. She was extremely happy to spend time with her brother Marco, who by now had memorized what he viewed as the most important quotes and passages from the book, *Think and Grow Rich.*

Marco told Gloria, "I truly believe my own 'burning desire' is not only to become rich, but also to believe in God.'"

Gloria was also quite impressed to hear that her father Luca had started joining her mother in going to church on Sundays. She reflected on the reality that her message of peace and love was radiating amongst the members of her own family already.

Halfway through her first year at the convent, Gloria decided there were a few questions she was eager to ask of Sister Delores. The two women agreed to meet during the break after lunch one day.

Gloria started the discussion by asking, "Sister Delores, I would like you to clarify an issue in my head. I very much love all that Jesus Christ said and did, and it is my intention to apply his teachings in my daily life. The issue I have is with the established institution of Christianity as a religion. Did Jesus create the religion, or was it St. Paul? I find it hard to believe that Jesus did. I find Jesus' message to be different than that of the organized Church. Please enlighten me.'"

Sister Delores looked pensive, and it is was only a good while later that she responded to the question.

"That is a very good question, Gloria, and one that has been on the mind of many scholars for centuries now. There is not one unified answer to your question that I know of. I personally choose to focus my life on Jesus' teachings first; the other rituals, rules and regulations of the church are secondary to me.

"Your question is the reason why we have so many different sects within Christianity: Diverse opinions on this topic inspired the creation of all the different schools of thought! It began with a rebellion against the rules of just one faith, and the person or people who rebelled went on to create another faith with a new set of rules. Such a thing went on and on—and now there is seemingly no end in sight!

"I personally believe that what has been going on during the last two thousand years is redundant. Power games by religious leaders have messed up the history of the church. Jesus never intend to create man-made power structures, so it is actually irrelevant to spend our time trying to figure out the right answer. What matters is to abide by His teachings and establish a one-on- one relationship with Him through the Holy Spirit. All the rest is secondary.'"

After listening attentively, Gloria said in an inquisitive tone, "I understand and I agree with much of what you have said. However, I also believe that such an attitude limits the expansion of Christ's teachings to a greater multitude of new believers. Something has to be done to attract those who love His teachings and get them to also accept the concept of church as well.

"I think further reforms of the old regulations and rituals ought to be introduced, and new seminars offering a more simplified message implemented. There continues to be bigger growth in terms of New Thought assemblies and other reformed churches than the growth going on within our own Catholic Church. You can call it 'competition', but it is definitely a race between various sects and religions to attract more members into their folds.'"

Clearly impressed by Gloria's knowledge and thought process, Sister Delores momentarily fidgeted in her chair, looked at the ceiling, and then said, "You may be right Gloria, but our problem here is that we must wait for new instructions to come from higher levels—for example, the Vatican—before any changes can be made. Yes, such changes have been made already, but as you may know, any change from old to new is not easy to implement. Complacency, or the fear of change, has produced the current stagnant situation in which we currently where we are. Anyhow, I appreciate your concern, and I hope you can come up with good ideas for improvement.'"

"I am far from being eligible to come up with any ideas at this point in time, but I definitely hope that one day I can figure out some ways that would empower people to abide by the great teachings of Jesus Christ on a daily basis. While I have your attention, may I inquire as to how open we are to accepting teachings from other religions?'"

"Our focus is to live by our Christian values, and if I may be candid, I am not well versed enough on the teachings of other religions to be able to give you an honest and knowledgeable response here.'"

"Do you mind, Sister Delores, if I share with you something I recently learnt? Of today's faiths, Christianity represents 32 percent of the world population, followed by Islam at 18 percent, Hinduism at 16 percent and Buddhism at 6 percent. The percentage of Agnostics and Atheists has risen to 16 percent, and the remaining balance of about 10 percent represents other traditional and minor religions. What is worth noticing is there has been a decline in Christian membership over the last two decades. My question is whether the reluctance of Christian leadership, and Catholics in particular, has anything to do with this decline?'"

"Yes, perhaps," Sister Delores acknowledged with a nod of her head. "I believe it will take people like you, Gloria, to bring about a change, or some kind of influence, that will allow us to revive and reclaim our Christian values and increase our membership.'"

"Sister Delores, thank you so much for this encouraging remark. I truly hope I can do so one day!'"

Gloria walked out from the Sister's office feeling good about herself and proud to be surrounded by such moral companions and teachers.

As the days passed, Gloria continued to immerse herself in the material provided by the courses she studied online. But she believed her main discoveries came from her new personal routine, designed to strengthen her inner being with divine guidance and insight. She derived incredible amount of joy and knowledge from the private prayers and meditations in her room.

Gloria had completely opened her heart to working on her desire to have an exciting future full of love, peace and happiness that she wanted to share with the rest of the world. She was doing everything she could to enhance the reality of this possibility.

As a young and driven Postulate, Gloria had a small following of admirers within the community of the convent. She simply had an inexplicable aura that attracted the attention of others.

Yet because Gloria had a humble approach and a loving attitude, there was no jealousy over her newfound popularity among her peers; rather, all respected her and sought her advice whenever they could. Several Novices and senior Sisters tried to persuade her not to leave the convent so soon, but Gloria was determined to move out into the world, to life outside the convent. She felt that as a good soldier, she ought to be serving others in the field now that she felt full of the insight and guidance derived from spending time with other faithful believers and the Holy Spirit while in the convent.

Gloria used this guidance and insight when spending time with the pregnant teenage girls who came to the convent seeking shelter. She spent an hour each day counseling one of the girls and hearing her individual story.

e young ladies, for them, After having counseled about twenty of the pregnant teenagers, Gloria realized the main reasons the girls became got pregnant arose from poverty and a lack of education. Some of the girls admitted to Gloria they did not know who the father of their unborn baby was, as they were either drunk or on drugs when they had sex.

Ironically, the teenage girls came from the nearby Bronx borough where Gloria had grown up.

Gloria had one more month of online studies before she concluded the second semester at the Seminary. She had learned a lot from the eight different courses she took on various subjects.

One particular course she took covered the rising modern spiritual movements around the world, with more than one hundred movements established in recent history. Sixty-five percent of these movements were not affiliated with Christianity in any way; instead, they were broadly diversified across all major world religions, and many also included fundamentalist, radical and occult organizations. Although this information widened Gloria's understanding, she was disturbed by the movements, themes, goals and potential influence on people's lives.

The other courses Gloria took gave her in-depth knowledge about the major religions, their history, their teachings and their continued activities. She learnt a lot about the evangelistic work of the disciples, and in particular Paul, who was instrumental in spreading the Gospel across new territories. Gloria also read several books and articles about the attempt to bring science and religion together as a new means of understanding a Cosmic God, the ultimate Universal Power.

Through her daily prayers and nightly conversations with the Holy Spirit, Gloria developed a strong personal relationship with Jesus Christ. After eight months of this dedicated work, Gloria heard a voice within telling her it was time to move out from the convent into the world without completing the full year residency. To clarify and discuss such thoughts, Gloria asked for another session with Sister Delores.

The session time was set for Sunday afternoon, after prayers in the chapel. This time the two women sat in a corner of the chapel after all the others had left.

Gloria turned to face Sister Delores and said to her in a low but clear voice, "I will not take a lot of your time, Sister Delores. I have been here for about eight months already, and it has been an amazing experience! It is the best time I have ever had in my life. I have learned a lot about our faith and our Lord, and also about my inner self and what I want to do in my life. I also increased my knowledge about other religions and the recent growth of new spiritual movements.

"I am thinking about moving out of the convent earlier than my original plan of one year— within a month, as this will coincide with the end of my second semester in school. I believe that I am ready to actively serve and do something constructive in the outside world. What do you think of this idea?'"

Sister Delores was taken by what she heard.

"Well, this sounds very interesting, Gloria, although I must admit I did not expect such news! I appreciate you confiding in me, and I do understand your eagerness to start your good deeds. Do you have any specific plans in mind?"

"I am thinking about asking my father to help me out financially so I can create centers in the Bronx to take care of teenage pregnant girls. I derived this inspiration from the counseling sessions I have had with the girls who have come to the convent for help. Most of them come from the Bronx, where my family home is. I have discovered that even though there are so many community centers in the Bronx area, there is only one center funded by the government that is a clinic to help out these helpless girls. That is not enough, given the high percentage of teenage pregnancies in the Bronx.'"

Gloria continued on with an excited tone in her voice. "I think it would be a good start to structure something a bit more comprehensive, but which is not necessarily a clinic. I am thinking about offering sex education programs, even for girls who are not pregnant. I also would introduce our Christian values to them, and teach them new skills to avoid the poverty that pushes them to get pregnant. I visualize several such centers with many volunteers and staff. This is my vision for the near future.'"

"Gloria, you are indeed a blessed soul. Follow your inspiration, and do what your inner voice tells you. We here at the convent will be available to extend any help you may need. Already we are so proud of you!'"

"Thank you, Sister Delores. I will talk the matter over with my father this coming weekend, and I leave it to you to discuss it with Mother Superior if you wish.'"

With that, Gloria walked briskly towards her room, feeling inspired and confident about her plan.

CHAPTER 5

The Beginning
of a Vision

G loria was young herself—only nineteen—but determined to go ahead with her plans to help pregnant teenagers. So when she went to visit her family the following weekend, she asked for some private time with her father. She wanted to discuss her inspired ideas with him and ask for financial backing before sharing the plan with her mom.

Luca received her in his study with open arms and a warm hug. When they sat down together, Gloria shared with him the highlights of her work and time at the convent. Then she went straight to the subject she intended to discuss with him.

"Father, I have a special request. First of all, let me tell you that the last eight months have been the best months of my life. I learned a lot, and I now know what I want, so I believe it is time for me to leave the convent soon. In about one month I will finish my second semester at the Seminary. I would like to establish centers here in the Bronx that would help to educate and counsel teenage girls. I met many of them who came to us at the convent; they are pregnant and helpless. I counseled many of them, and doing so is what inspired me to make my plan a reality in the near future. However, I would need your help financially to get started."'

Luca took a deep breath, and with a smile he said, "Wow, sweet Gloria! Your thoughtfulness and compassion is inspiring! Tell me how much and what you need."'

"Father, I actually don't know yet how much this might entail in terms of money. Perhaps you and my brother would have a better idea...? I need one physical location to start, either to rent or to buy. It would have be about three thousand square feet, with at least five to seven rooms in which to teach and shelter homeless girls. I also would need to fund salaries for an assistant, a nurse and a social worker. The rest of the staff could be comprised of volunteers.'"

"I am sure your brother and I can find the right space for you, Gloria, because of our real estate business and holdings. I will ask Marco to head up the search. I am more than happy to provide all the money you need to get this done, including paying for the salaries that might be necessary. In the meantime, I will ask my lawyer to register a non-profit organization in your name, unless you have a name picked out already. All should be ready by the time you come home.

"I am here for you, sweetheart, and you cannot imagine how proud you make me. You are truly a very honorable and caring person.'"

Gloria thanked her father, then went over and kissed him on the cheeks before she went to spend time with her mother and tell her the good news. The two of them decided on an early dinner, and to ask Marco and Maria to attend as well.

At dinner, they spoke about Gloria's plans. Marco assured her that he already had a place for her in mind, and that he would make sure it was ready within the month. He planned to approach an architect friend of his to do the design and furnishings.

After Gloria's left to return to the convent, the rest of the Camino family stayed around for two more hours talking about Gloria's plan. Luca, Luisa and Marco had an extremely spirited discussion, started by Luisa, who said to her husband, "Luca, it is definitely a great humanitarian idea that Gloria has, but don't you think it is somewhat...risky and dangerous?'"

Luca raised an eyebrow as he questioned, "Dangerous in what sense?'"

Luisa replied, "Often these pregnant teenage girls who are coming from poverty have been abused or drugged by their partners. The boys or the men who made them pregnant may well have violent tendencies. I am worried these men may disturb the work that Gloria plans to do and cause her trouble. We are so lucky to have her back, and I don't want anything untoward to happen to her again!'"

Luca gave his wife a reassuring smile. "Luisa, our daughter is an angel now, and no one will cause her any harm in the future. God will protect her now, and besides, she will always have people around her in the shelter.'"

Marco piped up, "Father, an easy solution that might keep Mom happy is to hire security guards 24/7 for the place. Our family is blessed with good resources, so the money for them should not be an issue.'"

Luca thought for a moment, then nodded his head in agreement. "Fine. If that will make you feel better, Luisa, it can be arranged. Our daughter plans to do unbelievable work, so let us support her and help her in whatever way we can. I actually bet you this is only the start for her! I am sure she has even greater ideas brewing in her head. Our Gloria is unstoppable. Let us all go to sleep now feeling good about her great news.'"

The following day Mother Superior summoned Gloria.

Gloria felt a bit apprehensive when she received the request. She thought, *Perhaps Sister Delores had already briefed Mother Superior on my plan to leave the convent sooner than originally planned, and she is going to ask me to hold back on making this decision!*

However, Gloria kept her worrisome thoughts to herself as she went to Mother Superior's office accompanied by Sister Delores.

Mother Superior greeted Gloria with a hug, then sat back down behind her desk.

"Gloria, I hear from Sister Delores you have some interesting ideas that are prompting you to leave us sooner than expected. Is that correct?'"

"Yes, Mother Superior. I have a burning desire I must make a reality, and my idea of opening centers to help pregnant teenage girls was inspired by my service to them here in this convent! I am very grateful to have had that experience while here.

"When I spoke to many of them I learned they mostly come from the Bronx, which is where I grew up and where my family still lives.'"

"How certain are you that you will succeed without any hurdles or trouble from the boys or men who made them pregnant? Here they are safe, but if they continue to reside where their troubles started, who knows?'"

"Actually, Mother Superior, my mother had the same concern when I visited my family yesterday and told them my news," Gloria confided. "But my father and my brother have reassured her that they would pay for security guards on the premises around the clock. My father also agreed to provide me with an appropriate space, and to pay for all the expenses involved in setting up and running the center. They are all enthused about the idea, and promised to do their best to help.'"

"What services will you provide these girls, Gloria?" Mother Superior asked as she assumed a more relaxed posture.

"First, there will be a space big enough for them to use as a temporary shelter in which to sleep. I will counsel them and educate them about the love of Christ, and also to have hope that all will be well. I will feed them and arrange for them to stay until I can find for them the right professional place to go to next. I will search for foster homes and jobs when it is required. My plan is to have a full-time nurse, a administrative assistant, and a part-time social worker at the new shelter.'"

"But Gloria, you are only nineteen! Are you sure you can manage all this?" Mother Superior asked, her eyes probing Gloria's.

"Yes, Mother, by the Grace of God I will manage. You provided me with a good education here, and my relationship with God has become so strong that I have no fear or hesitation about doing the work. And I also plan to continue my online studies through the Seminary.'"

"Well, Gloria, I have not come across a beautiful soul quite like yours in all my years here in this convent! I am elated by this news of your plans, and I bless them all. As a small contribution from the convent, I plan to send you one Sister every day of the week to help you with the chores at your center. They all know you already, and they love you as I do. I hope to visit you one day when you are settled in.'"

"Thank you so much, Mother Superior, and I am so grateful for your generous offer," Gloria answered with teary eyes.

Mother Superior rose from her chair and turned towards Gloria, giving her a hug from all her heart.

Word about Gloria's plan swiftly spread around the convent. The nuns gathered for their usual prayer session, but afterwards, they all waited around for the chance to talk to Gloria and congratulate her.

During their breaks, the younger candidates approached Gloria and asked if they should leave themselves to go join her in her work. Gloria advised them to pray to discover out their particular calling first. While she expressed her gratitude for their willingness to help, she asked them not to rush before they really knew what they want to do with their own future.

When Gloria went to her room in the evening, she was full of joy: All signs led to go forward with purpose. She rested in bed for a while to reflect on the events of the last twenty-four hours and felt good about where she was at in her life. Later, she got up, sat at her desk and opened her journal that by now was almost full from all her reflections during the last eight months. She wrote:

> *I am so blessed. Now I know the purpose for my existence on this planet. I prayed and <u>asked</u> for guidance, I <u>believed</u> in what I wanted to do, and now God has <u>answered</u>. The door is wide open now, and everybody I know wants to help in my new project. They all trust me and believe I will succeed. I am so encouraged by their support and truly feel their love.*
>
> *Hebrews13:16 says:*
>
> *"Do not neglect to do good and to share what you have, for such sacrifices are pleasing to God."*
>
> *For myself I visualize a future full of wonderful surprises and unexpected results. I see the work I am planning expanding to the creation of more centers in other areas of the Bronx, and hopefully even beyond that! I see donations pouring in, and many young girls receiving an education that helps them to stay out from trouble. I will teach these young girls new skills, and help them to believe in God and themselves.*
>
> *I will continue my religious studies and continue to learn until I find the way to spread my message of love, peace and joy to the world.*

Gloria slept very peacefully that night. She was fully aligned with her inner being. Her inspired thoughts matched well with her positive feelings about the success of her mission.

A few days later Marco called his sister at the convent. His voice sounded excited as he said, "Little sister, I have come up with the right space for your work! It is a building our family owns, and it is located on a fairly good street in the northeastern part of the Bronx. The building consists of three floors, and is about a ten-minute drive from home. The spaces on the street level are rented out to several retailers already. The second and third levels are empty, however, for we were about to rent them out as offices. The space of the two upper levels combined is about 3,800 square feet. Father has agreed to leave the spaces available to you so you may do your shelter work.

"There is a private entrance to the space, and there is a solid front door and an intercom system for buzzing in any visitors that should make you feel more secure in the space.'"

"This is great news, Marco," Gloria said enthusiastically. "When will all be ready?'"

"The architect needs about one month to design and connect the two floors together. On the lower level I told him to provide for an office and a conference room, two smaller rooms for consultations, restrooms, a dining area and a kitchen. On the upper level there will be seven small bedrooms, and a large shared bathroom. If we put two single beds in each room, there will be enough space for fourteen girls to sleep and live on a temporary basis. What do you think?'"

"Marco, this is beyond my expectations. Thank you and Dad so much for your love and attention to the task at hand!"

"Gloria, what you are doing is transforming all of our lives—not just yours—in the right direction. You set such a good example, and we can only thank God our family has the financial means to help you get started. The lawyer is registering the organization under the name, 'Gloria's Mercy Centers.' You can change that if you want a different name for your centers.'"

"That name is fine for now. Thanks again, and I will come down to visit you next week even though I will be out of here within two weeks' time.'"

Diana, another Postulate and by now quite a good friend of Gloria's, asked to speak with her one afternoon during the break after lunch.

With a sincere tone in her voice, Diana looked straight into Gloria's eyes as she articulated, "Gloria, since our last talk I have been thinking and praying about what I want to do with my life. Thanks to God—and to you, by the way—I am now over my emotional crisis. I also know I really do not see myself spending the rest of my life as a nun here in the convent. I would love to remain close to you, for I admire your clarity of mind and the goodness of your soul. I have learned it is my desire to help you in your new project and become your administrative assistant. I will do whatever you want me to do, and I wanted to tell you I don't need to be paid if you allow me to live and eat on the premises. Please consider my offer.'"

"Diana, you are so sweet to make this offer! You have come a long way in overcoming your emotional upset since we first met, do good work in this world.

"In my short time here, I have noticed how you have helped the pregnant teenage girls wholeheartedly. You are punctual in attending all our group prayers and activities, and y You have become a good friend, and a strong person inside and out. I am flattered by your offer, and I will think about it. I will let you know as soon as I can.'"

"Thank you, Gloria. And please let me say that what you are doing for someone your age is unheard of. You should be so proud.'"

"Diana, I am just doing what I am guided to do. I connect with my inner voice and I listen to the messages I receive from the Supreme Soul. I am just a messenger, and I am honored to perform these tasks to help others.'"

In the last week at the convent, Gloria prepared for an online exam of a course she had found extremely enlightening. The course was about Quantum Physics and Spirituality.

Gloria had learned that the belief that science and religion were completely separate and held no commonality had been changing. For years there had been a 'tug of war' between science and religion; a person was either a man of God, or a man of science, and there was no middle ground. But quantum physics was shedding new light on people's understanding of God and how the Universe was created:

"We are really beings of energy and vibration, radiating our own unique energy signature."

More and more people were accepting a merger of, or a blurring of, what had been once two separate schools of thought! People were yearning to live by the unification of body, soul and mind. They believed they could become one with the Universe, or one with God.

Quantum physics held that people are interconnected, for although people are different forms of energy, all are derived from the energy field of the Universe. Quantum physics was demystifying the process of Creation, for it was believed that man's thoughts, beliefs and emotions were shaping the world in which people lived. Man was not separate anymore from the Universe, so it was simple for man to have conscious manifestations.

Many of the new schools of thought now believed in science as a contemporary spirituality. Many New Thought churches were surfacing, and embellishing upon the teachings of Christ in their new philosophies. Such churches also emphasized the power of mind over body. Too, the growth of those joining these New Thought churches was significant; these churches were attracting more and more members, while the membership in the traditional old churches was declining.

This new wave of spirituality sweeping the nation and the world was in line with Gloria's own thinking about the future of Christianity and the other main religions!

And deep within her, Gloria still sensed that soft voice expressing its desire to revive the original, but increasingly dormant, teachings of Christ.

So Gloria decided to expand her knowledge by taking additional online courses through the Seminary for at least another year. She realized that it might take her few more years to acquire the necessary knowledge and experience that would enable her to communicate her message to the masses.

For now, what was most pressing was to start her Center for pregnant teens, and to learn about life from the experiences of others. She was looking forward to putting 'love in action into practice!'

Before she fell asleep that night, Gloria thought about the name of the new centers and what her response to Diana should be. She decided to take her name out of the organization, and just call it, 'Mercy Centers'. She also decided to accept Diana as her assistant. She decided to tell Marco to make one of the rooms to have one bed only placed in it. This would be Diana's room.

The next morning, Gloria called Marco and told him about the name change and the room intended for Diana. She also told Diana that she was accepting her generous offer.

With only a few days left before Gloria moved out of the convent, Mother Superior arranged a farewell gathering to wish Gloria well. Gloria's eyes teared up at the sight of a large cake decorated with her name on it.

One by one the Sisters came to say goodbye to Gloria and wish her great success with her project. A few shed tears as they discussed how much she will be missed.

Gloria promised to drop by and visit the convent every now and then over the months to come.

And so, on the next Saturday afternoon, Gloria's nine months at the convent ended, along with her second semester of her online education. Her parents came to drive Gloria and her few belongings home. Before they left the grounds of the convent, they extended their thanks to Sister Delores and Mother Superior, who walked with them to the parking lot to wave goodbye.

At home, there was a reception for Gloria. It was a feast to celebrate Gloria's return to the 'real world' and to congratulate her on her new venture.

Maria organized the party, along with the help of her husband and her brother Marco. Maria made sure to invite all the members of their extended family, as well as some close family friends.

Marco's friend the architect was there as well, and he showed Gloria the plans for her new space. Gloria had no prior experience with these kinds of plans, so she readily agreed to almost all that he had designed. She also told him how grateful she was that some of the work had already gotten started.

A little later, Luca told his daughter that the non-profit organization was about to be officially registered, and he confirmed that his lawyer had revised the organization's name per her request. He said he had targeted the opening date to be in about thirty days, at the start of summer.

Gloria hugged her father upon hearing this news, then said she planned to go see the space for herself on the upcoming Monday.

At this point, Maria asked if she might speak with Gloria in private. Gloria's sister took her to a quiet corner and said to her, "Dear Gloria, we have not had a chance to talk privately, just you and me. And I wanted to tell you that I am highly impressed by your life choices. I took it for granted that you would follow in my footsteps, marry and have children. Evidently, you have chosen a different life for yourself, and I admire the independent path you're on and your charitable decisions.'"

"Thank you for such kind words, Maria! I believe it is all right that we are choosing such different paths for our life journeys. We are sisters from the same parents, but two independent souls. I believe our destiny was already written for us before we were born, and I better understand now why I did not like to go out on dates or to parties when I was younger. That kind of life was not meant to be mine! I tell you I have never been happier in my life that I am right now, for now I really know what I want.'"

"That is so great to hear, Gloria, but don't forget your older sister in the future! You know how much I love you, so feel free to ask me for any help you may need.'"

The two sisters hugged before rejoining the party.

Then Luca requested Gloria's attention yet again.

Father and daughter walked to his office, and after the two sat down on the sofa there, Luca asked in a gentle voice, "How does it feel to be back home, sweetheart?'"

"I am thrilled to be with the family again, Dad, and I want to thank you again for your wonderful support and understanding of what I am about to do. The past nine months have taught me a great deal about myself and my purpose. I also am so blessed to have a family who can afford to help me out, and who wants to do so. All of you will be rewarded with plenty of abundance, joy and good health for your generous actions and love.'"

"If I know you well, Gloria, I don't think you will be satisfied with just one Center. So I want to ask you to please let me know whenever you are guided to start another center. You are giving me the opportunity, through funding the initial center, to contribute back to this community.

"Gloria, I also plan to raise funds for the Center in the future from the many friends of mine who owe me a financial 'raincheck,'" Luca chuckled. "Your character and future plans have uplifted my soul, and revived my faith in God. So it is truly *I* who should be thanking *you,* my dear!'"

At this point Marco, who had been looking for his sister, found Gloria in his father's study.

"I hope I am not interrupting!" he called in from the entrance leading into his father's office.

"No, no, come on in, Marco," Luca urged.

"Gloria, I have been looking for you. I wanted to say that I can't thank you enough for the book you gave me. I have read it again and again and again! Not only it is teaching me how to succeed by changing my thoughts and feelings, but it has also introduced me to a greater value system altogether. As a result of the insight the book has given me, I have changed my manner of speech and the way I used to think! I also have learned how to focus on holding positive feelings about myself and the rest of the world. You are my hero, little sister!'"

Gloria jumped off the sofa to hug him, so touched was she by his words.

The siblings' father decided to join in the hug as well. As he wrapped his beefy arms around his children, Luca spouted tears of joy in his eyes. He could not help reflect on the wonderful recent transformation in his family—due to Gloria's influence!

Gloria went with Marco on Monday to see the space for her new project. She was taken aback by its considerable size and prime location.

When she went to the second level, she came across several workers busy cleaning debris from the demolishment of previous walls, as well as a big open space which she recognized would be divided into different rooms as per the architect's plan.

When Gloria and Marco visited the third floor, she discovered the upstairs space was already cleaned up and awaiting the architect's arrival of the architect before dividing it into bedrooms and bathrooms.

As they walked the premises, Marco told Gloria he would have his accountant come over once a week to keep the organization's books in order. Gloria thanked him, then mentioned she was reluctant to have a security guard posted at the location. So Marco suggested he install an alarm system for the space instead, in addition having an intercom by the main door. Gloria approved he revised plan.

All in all, Marco was delighted to see how happy Gloria was with the location and the plans.

Once back at the Camino mansion, Gloria started planning how to send word out to the community about the Center and its purpose. She wanted to notify the hospitals and clinics in the nearby area about her work, and ask for volunteers from their staff. But she was interrupted by a call from Diana, who told her that Mother Superior had agreed to release her in thirty days to join Gloria's center.

When Gloria got off the call, she decided to started working with a web designer on creating a website for the Center to explain its purpose and its location. She thought it would be great if her site was linked to other official sites related to the same purposes.

Gloria was very excited about her new venture, and in the time before the Center opened, she started researching and reading many articles to learn how to better manage a place like this and the girls who would be treated on the premises.

In her reading Gloria discovered that it was likely for practically all the teenage girls who came to her center to have serious emotional issues. Chances are they would have been mistreated, and abused both physically and emotionally. The majority of such cases would hail from poor backgrounds, and most of the girls would have had very little schooling and education.

Gloria realized the challenge ahead was big, but she had no fear or hesitation about moving forward. If she was planning correctly, she hoped her Center would treat about eighty girls in its first year of operation.

CHAPTER 6

Mercy and Attraction

Thirty days later, Gloria opened the door to her first Mercy Center. The facility was clean and ready for action. The space was fully furnished, and the architect had designed a comfortable office and an adjacent conference room for Gloria, staff and the visitors to use. The new intercom also featured a camera that would show who was at the door asking to be buzzed in.

Gloria showed Diana her spacious room upstairs, and Diana was elated to be by Gloria's side helping out in the new venture.

Gloria had already contacted and made arrangements with various institutes and hospitals in the community to be ready to accept the girls she would send to them for long-term care. She was not running a clinic, but a temporary transit that offered initial counseling and care for those who were homeless and had nowhere else to go.

During the Center's first day of operation, there were two cases admitted. The first, a sixteen-year-old girl, was five months pregnant, and she had run away from home, for her mother was a drunk. She told Gloria she had no idea who the father of her unborn baby was, as she herself had used to drink a lot, and she had slept with many different boys. She had never learned how to read and write, and she looked very weak and tired.

Diana took her upstairs so she could shower first. Then she gave her a new set of underwear and a hospital-type robe to wear. Gloria had stocked a bunch of such items on the premises, knowing that the girls would not arrive here

Then Diana compassionately told the girl she would be safe here, and it was time for her rest on a bed and get some much-needed sleep.

The other girl was eighteen, and while she was not pregnant, she had come in seeking shelter from a boyfriend who was violent and emotionally abusive. She opened her heart to Gloria right away, sharing horrible stories of how she had been abused by her boyfriend. She explained to Gloria that Joey was a drug addict who had forced her to do drugs with him.

She told Gloria she was very lucky she was not gotten pregnant, and then began sobbing when she asked Gloria if she could stay at the Center for few days until she sobered up.

After an hour of counseling, Gloria asked Diana to help the young lady clean up, and bring her to rest upstairs.

After admitting the first two girls into the Center, Gloria and Diana sat down together in the main office. They began holding their hands in supplication as they asked God for continued guidance and support. After, the two smiled at each other, for each now felt confident that they could handle whatever came their way.

Around noon, Diana went to the kitchen to prepare sandwiches and glasses of water to give the girls.

Since no one rang the doorbell that day, Gloria stayed in her office checking out the new courses offered during her next semester at the Seminary. She also continued to read and study programs that dealt with teenage pregnancies and how to manage them.

She already realized from the material she had studied previously that her Center should only provide short-term care; each individual case would be different from another, so it would be her job to decide on whether to transfer the girls to a particular professional institute or a hospital for more long-term care. Gloria's Center was not licensed to provide long-term care, and the intention was not to open a health clinic with licensed doctors and nurses. The program at Mercy Center was to provide temporary relief and rest, done with love and counseling. The plan was that the Center would provide care for few days, or a couple of weeks at the most. Arrangements would then be made for the girls at the appropriate long-term healthcare centers within the community.

When the Center's first two girls were awake and rested, Diana asked them to fill out admission forms, which should include: their names, parents' names and phone numbers, home address, name and contact details of any boyfriend or father of the baby, schools they may have attended, and hospitals or names of doctors they may have visited before. Questions were asked if they knew of any diseases they had contracted and any medications they have taken. Diana explained that guests at the Center were required to sign these forms, as they would also release the Center or its caretakers from any liability.

The next day, Sister Delores called Gloria to tell her told her that a Novice will come to help out at the Center the next day. The police department called later that afternoon to say they would be sending over three girls who needed help the next day. Gloria was fine with this number of girls, as the Center now offered room for up to twelve girls in its six available rooms. But frankly, Gloria was happy that a nun would be there to help out the next day with all the newcomers. As excited as Gloria was, she could not help but be a bit nervous, as all of this was new to her. Fortunately, she had mastered her ability to go within when needed, and align her self with her inner being for continued energy and positive hopes.

The young girls who arrived in a police all were from the Bronx. The youngest was fifteen, while the other two were seventeen and nineteen.

The nineteen-year-old was in bad shape: She was not pregnant, but she was so stoned she could hardly stand straight. Diana took her upstairs right away to sleep it off, knowing the best course of action was to wait before asking the young lady to fill out an admittance form. The younger ones were both pregnant and needed shelter. Gloria helped them fill out and sign their forms.

Gloria then talked to one girl, and Diana the other, in the Center's conference room. The girl's stories were pretty much alike in that they had no idea how they got pregnant, and they had mothers who were alcoholics. Both Gloria and Diana reassured them that God loves them, and not to worry; they would be receiving the care and love they deserved at the Center.

When Gloria left the Center at eight o'clock, she left all five girls with Diana, who managed to get them to go to sleep early after they took showers and had something to eat.

Gloria locked the door to the Center as she left. She had instructed Diana not to open it up to anybody in the middle of the night, and to call her in case of any emergency.

Once home, an exhausted Gloria told her family about the events of the day and said she would be going to bed early to rest. Before she went to sleep, though, she opened her journal and wrote:

>*This has been an eventful day at the Center! We received five girls already, and all need help and counseling. I will start requesting volunteers to show up and help us out during the day. Perhaps my mother can ask the people in her church to consider volunteering their time? It is evident I will be very busy, and I need to find time to continue my studies online, for they start within one week.*
>
>*I am grateful to Diana and for all the help from the convent. This new experience will widen my horizons, and enlighten my search for a meaningful and productive future. I pray for guidance on how to handle these girls tomorrow.*

Luca was downstairs in his study talking to Luciano, who had called him to find out if he can be of help in any way to his family. Clearly he was still seeking to make amends for his son's misguided actions.

Luca said thoughtfully, "Well, Luciano, maybe you can help out Gloria! She has opened a 'Mercy Center' for troubled pregnant teenage girls from the Bronx. If you want to help, you can either donate cash to her non-profit organization, or find her some volunteers willing to help out during the day.'"

Luciano immediately promised, "I will do both.'"

Luciano was true to his word! Three days later Gloria's organization received a donation of $50,000. That same day, a middle-aged woman named Norma showed up on the front steps of the organization. Once she was buzzed in, she explained to Gloria that she was a friend of Luciano's who had worked as a registered nurse in a hospital. She was recently retired, and would love to work in the center as a volunteer.

Gloria welcomed Norma, and told her that her presence would truly be helpful in assessing the condition of the girls' health and providing the girls with any necessary healthcare before they were transferred to a professional clinic or hospital for further treatment.

After this meeting, Gloria called Luciano to express her gratitude for his generous donation, as well as Norma's referral. She also added that she was praying for Andrea.

By the end of the first week, the Center had checked in eight girls in total. Two of the girls were scheduled to move out before the end of the second week: Gloria had made arrangements for one to go to a rehab center, and another to a health clinic sponsored by the government. As for the young fifteen-year-old, she would be going to live in a foster home in the near future.

There were no untoward incidents in the Center, and the girls told Gloria they appreicated the care and counseling they received.

The first month went by, and still the operation was running smoothly! About nineteen people had walked into the Center. Seven had left soon thereafter to receive long-term care in their designated location. There were still twelve girls on the premises, so the Center was filled to capacity.

While the girls lived on the premises, they were required to participate in housekeeping chores that included cleaning and laundry. Additionally, they were taught how to cook and prepare food in the kitchen. They Center wanted to actively encourage the girls to learn new skills to help them earn a living and become independent in the future.

Each day every girl received a two-hour counseling session. They were all taught about God, and how to pray.

Gloria had hoped she could provide the girls with even more help and guidance, but the teenagers could only stay at the Center for a limited period of time.

Over the next six months, people donated enough money to the Center that there was a sufficient amount to take care of all operating expenses. Nevertheless, being the driven young lady that she was, Gloria was thinking about establishing another Mercy Center. She hoped to have enough money to do so without bothering her father or brother any more.

The new online courses Gloria selected from the Seminary's offerings that semester were quite different than her previous ones. She was choosing to focus more on modern spirituality, and how that differed in practice and belief from the old established religions. She was eager to find out more about the new wave of spirituality wherein people, especially those of the younger generation, were apt to refer to themselves as 'spiritual, but not religious.'

She also took another course to learn more about the impact of quantum physics on religious beliefs. She aspired to find out why there was such a huge interest in the Universal Law of Attraction and its very popular manifestation in the documentary, 'The Secret.'

After researching this matter more, Gloria asked her brother Marco one evening if she could have a thorough discussion with him on the Law of Attraction, which he had been bringing up in brieffor several weeks over the dinner table.

The two sat down in the family's living room, and Gloria told him she was taking courses in this new field of 'practical spirituality,' as some referred to it.

Marco replied in a serious voice, "I am very happy to hear you are opening yourself up to such new knowledge, little sister!'"

"Marco, are you able to tell me why you think this new wave of spirituality is rising at the expense of diminished interest in established religions?'"

"Actually, Gloria, I do not feel this new wave is in contradiction to, or opposed to, the Christian faith and beliefs. The truth is, I actually believe it could enhance Christianity so that its followers go on to reach higher levels of understanding about who they are in relation to God, or the Supreme Source of energy.'"

"How so, Marco?'"

"Well, you and I grew up as Catholics who believed we had to accept whatever the priests taught us. We did not have the freedom to question the established doctrines. This discouraged many followers like us from seeking out explanations about God, the Universe, and The Bible.

As a result, many started searching elsewhere. The advent of quantum physics in the last century facilitated a lot of the ambiguity hidden in religions. There are several new books that I would recommend for you read if you are interested to learn more about the new modern spirituality.'"

"Which ones would you recommend, my 'genius' brother Marco? So I want to read up more on the matter. I also want you to know how impressed I am about the noticeable change in your character. Your thoughts and feelings have become so positive, and that delights me!"

"Don't forget that it was you who started my transformation, Gloria! You're the who gave me the book, *Think and Get Rich,* and I considers its author, Napoleon Hill, to be the father of the Law of Attraction. So as for recommendation, if you have not yet read *The Secret* already, please do so.

Another book I recommend is *The Law of Attraction* by Esther and Jerry Hicks. They explain it with clarity and offer a practicality of application. Once you are done with those two works, I will introduce you to some of the other schools of thought."

"I don't know why I should study in school anymore, Marco; I have you instead, my dear professor," Gloria said with laughter in her voice.

"I am flattered, my dear little sister whose dreams are bigger than Mount Everest!" Marco teased in return. "How is your Center doing, and what are your future plans?'"

"We have been quite busy at the Center; we have handled about twenty cases of young girls who needed help thus far. I am blessed to have three ladies assisting me now, including a nun whom the convent sends to me every day. We also are well financed, thanks in particular to a big donation from Luciano, Andrea's father, and other friends of our father.

"Don't laugh now, but I am planning to open a second Mercy Center soon! I wish to have two Centers open by the time I turn twenty.'"

"What a blessed soul you are, Gloria! I am so proud of you, and I am there for you, especially if you need further education for free on how to get rich and successful," Marco teased. "Just kidding! I love you very much, and you have become the pride of our family.'"

"Marco, I have out found the reason why I am here on this planet, and now I am working on fulfilling the purpose behind that reason. Without purpose, my life becomes meaningless.'"

"So you no longer want to be a nun?'"

"My journey calls me to be 'in the field;' I have a different calling! With what I do now, I practice unconditional love. I am free to create my own reality, and to align my vibrations and feelings with my inner being. I am one with myself.'"

"Wow, Gloria, these are the same kinds of words and beliefs that you find in books about the Law of Attraction. You are definitely a good candidate to excel in this field of practical spirituality. In fact, I am certain I will be seeing you writing books about this subject; you are a natural!'"

"I am not worried about my future, Marco; I know it will be full of unknown possibilities. I focus on the now, and on the task at hand. The future will unfold on its own speed and time. As for now, may I invite you to come visit me at the Center sometime?'"

"Yes, and thank you for our enlightening conversation. Before I forget, try to read the book, *Ask and It is Given,* also by Esther and Jerry Hicks. It explains to you how you can manifest your desires to live a joyous life.'"

So impressed was Gloria to hear about her brother's new spiritual journey and advice that as soon as she went to her room she went online and ordered the books that Marco had recommended.

CHAPTER 7

The Second Manifestation

Gloria arrived at the Center around eight a.m. to find Diana downstairs already with the girls having breakfast. They all looked happy and rested, even though apparently there had been a mild incident around midnight the night before.

Diana told Gloria that there was a loud knock on the door; after that, the doorbell was ringing non-stop.

"I got up to see who it was," Diana explained, "and I used the intercom; I did not open the door, for I did not know who it was. It was a young man asking to see Emma, and I politely asked him to leave. He refused and said he would stay there all night at our entrance until she came out. I did not want to bother you so late, so I called the police. They were here five minutes later, and they took him away.'"

Emma stood up from her seat at the dining table to say, "I am very sorry, Miss Gloria, for the noise he caused that woke us all up! He must have found out somehow that I came here yesterday.

"I ran away from my boyfriend, Jared, because he is abusive to me. Most of the time now he comes home high and drunk. He gets furious over nothing, and he uses that as an excuse to beat me up. I didn't call the police on him when it started because I loved him, and I hoped he would stop.

"Jared is twenty and works in construction. I am eighteen, and trying to finish my high school diploma, for I really want to do something meaningful in life. He and I thought we had it all at first, but the alcohol has changed him a lot. When he was sober, he is a different person, but lately it is so rare for me to see him sober. I don't know where to go now if you were to ask me to leave because of him coming by and disturbing everyone like this.'"

"Relax, Emma, it is all right and not your fault," Gloria reassured her. "How he treats you is the reason we are here, and we want to help you escape such treatment. I will check with the police to see where he is now, and so I'll need you to give me his full name. We will attempt to figure out a solution to your situation, but it is unfortunate that we can only house you on a temporary basis. For now, continue on with your day as planned by Diana, and we will talk more in depth later."

When she got to her office, Gloria called her father and told him Emma's story, since She gave the name of the man that caused the disturbance so that Luca could call his friend and ask him to check on Jared's status.

A few minutes after Luca talked with the police chief, the chief called him back and said, "The man is still being held by the police. He was put him behind bars because he was drunk and causing some sort of a disturbance."

Luca explained what happened at the Center in detail and implored his friend, "Chief, please keep an eye on his case! He could bother his girlfriend again at the Center, and that won't go over well in the neighborhood."

The chief assured him, "I will keep him in custody until the officers in charge are satisfied he will not do such a thing again.

I also will have some of my officers patrol the area of the Center at nighttime in the future to ensure that that the staff and girls do not have to worry about anyone bothering them overnight."

"Thank you, my friend," Luca told the police chief before he called Gloria and briefed her on the conversation.

Gloria then called Emma to come to her office.

"Emma, I've decided you can stay here so long as you want so long until we are sure Jared is going to behave himself. You will be happy to hear my father ha spoken with the local police chief. We've been assured that Jared will be monitored and/or put on some sort of probation. In fact, Jared may have to join AA, or go into rehab. Meanwhile, you should stay here with us, and I will find some kind of work for you to do while you are here."

"Thank you, thank you! I will do whatever you ask me to do. I can clean the floors and the toilets, I can cook, and I can do accounting work too! I promise to be a good role model to the other girls. I am a good listener, and compassionate."

"That is wonderful, Emma! Now go ahead with your schedule for the day."

When she ran into Diana later on the premises, Gloria also told her that Emma was smart, polite, and educated, and that it seemed possible Emma could become a member of the staff at the Center one day.

The Center remained full. Day after day it was abuzz with conversations and laughter, evidence of a jovial environment created by the help of the staff members. New girls kept coming to stay the moment there was space available for them at the Center, and Gloria kept the police notified in advance about when any vacancies would available.

Norma, the Center' nurse, kept close tabs on three of the pregnant girls who were in a bit of pain and discomfort. They were required them to rest on their backs for most of the day.

Meanwhile, the convent's visiting nun put into daily practice a Bible study group with six of the girls to teach them God's love, along with their need to love themselves as well.

Gloria found it extremely difficult to push girls o, to another facility if they still needed help, whether it be physical or emotional. The girls who did move on to other professional places always left with tears in their eyes. They truly appreciated the love and care they had received at Mercy Center, and generally expressed to the staff how much they would miss those at the Center.

Many of the young women bonded well with the other girls who had also sought shelter, so much so that several decided to stay in touch with each other after leaving to provided much needed support.

Gloria engaged the services of Emma a month after observing her behavior and work ethics. It turned out Emma was quite capable of handling the nonprofit's books, so Marco was able to stop sending his accountant to assist.

Emma was also quite good at talking with the girls about their emotional turmoil, especially as she had been in the same situation herself. So it wasn't long before Gloria began to consider Emma a fourth helper at the Center.

As for Emma's one-time boyfriend Jared, he was attending AA. meetings on a regular basis. Jared started Emma letters at the Center, for he was not allowed to go visit her there himself. In the letters he expressed his apologies for mistreating her before, and promised her that he would continue to go to AA meetings for a few more months.

After receiving a half-dozen or so letters from Jared, Emma met with Gloria. In a hopeful but hesitant voice she asked, "Could I see him for an hour one day sometime soon, to assess his condition and to see first-hand if he is truly making the progress he claims in his letters?"

Gloria considered the look on Emma's face.

"I see that you still have a great deal of love for this man. Emma, while it is good to forgive, I feel that a meeting at this time should be supervised. Any progress of Jared's is very recent, so see if you can arrange to meet him at a nearby coffee shop. I will ask Diana to accompany you as a safety measure; she can sit at another table and watch over you during this time."

"That is a great plan! It is so very kind of you, Miss Gloria."

"Promise me that you will not give him false hopes, Emma. I truly feel he has to stick to his AA. program for quite a bit longer for it to effect real change."

"I promise you I will not, and thank you again. You are the best."

A few days later, Emma and Jared met, with Diana looking on.

Emma felt Jared looked better than he had in recent months. For his part, Jared told Emma he had not touched alcohol for more than a month. He told Emma how much he loved her and wanted her in his life, and that he was willing to wait for her to suggest their next meeting.

Gloria was enjoying reading the books about the Law of Attraction. She was impressed by the contents of the two books written by Esther and Jerry Hicks, and found out Esther was channeling the answers from a guided spirit, Abraham, to questions asked.

After she finished the book, Gloria wondered if she had also been chosen by the Holy Spirit to communicate messages to the public.

Moreover, Gloria was learning from the Seminary's courses that there are other schools of spiritual teachings to help people to live a better life. By now Gloria fully understood how the cooperative relationship between a person's positive thoughts and feelings created that person's reality and personality. Once created, it then attracted magnetically other similar thoughts.

What Gloria liked very much was Napoleon Hill's definition of faith: *'Faith is the eternal elixir which gives life, power and action to the impulses of thought.'* She found this statement complementary to the concept of faith she had developed through practicing Christianity. Napoleon Hill had clarified his definition further through writing, *'Faith is the element which transforms the ordinary vibration of thought, into the spiritual equivalent.'*

In brief, Gloria felt that these books and courses confirmed that modern spirituality had evolved from taking place in a stagnant religious setting— something she herself had experienced earlier in her life—to an active and engaged way of living in the here and now. Through acquiring this new knowledge, Gloria could now sense and taste the beauty of good thoughts and great feelings.

Gloria also discovered all the New Thought churches were spreading similar messages of spirituality, to encourage individuals to have a direct spiritual experience with the Source of all Intelligence and the creator of the Universe, God.

Three full months passed since the Center opened, and in that time about thirty-six girls with different needs were supported, with the average stay for each girl being about eight days. So Gloria's target of helping about eighty cases for the year did not seem farfetched. Gloria decided it was time to start searching for a second space in the southern part of the Bronx.

Since the Camino family's real estate business was mostly versed in the northern region of the Bronx, Luca thought that perhaps Luciano, who ran his business in South Bronx, could help find a good space for another Center.

Luca called Luciano and asked if he could recommend a place.

A mere two hours later, Luciano called Luca to say, "Luca, I own a building located on the main street. I would be delighted to offer use of it to Gloria. It is one big level of about 4,500 square feet. What do you think?

"It sounds good, Luciano. When will it be available?'"

"In about four months. It is currently rented to a financial company that outgrew the space and is moving into Manhattan.'"

"Thank you, Luciano," Luca responded, thrilled that the search seemed to be over so quickly. "I will inform Gloria."

Luca called Gloria and told her. She was excited to hear about the offer, and called Luciano herself to ask if she could go see it with Marco and his friend the architect. Luciano said yes.

Two days later Gloria, accompanied by Marco and the architect, went to see the space still occupied by the financial company. After they walked the length of the building, the architect said it would be easy to design and renovate, especially since all the offices on the floor were removable cubicles. He said the space could easily fit twenty beds in ten rooms that would be placed in the back of the space. The part of the building fronting the main street would be sufficient to accommodate the office spaces, dining area and kitchen.

Upon hearing this good report, Gloria pulled out her phone and called Luciano to ask, "What is the rent I need to calculate for this space? It looks like a perfect spot for a new Mercy Center!'"

"Gloria, the normal rent is twelve dollars a square foot, but I am going to offer it to you for your Center for exactly half that amount. Is that doable for your organization?"

Without hesitation Gloria replied, "Thank you, sir, for your generosity, and I will manage by God's grace! I agree to the terms."

Gloria had true faith that paying the rent would not become an issue for the Center. When she turned to tell Marco and the architect, Marco was speechless for a moment, so stunned was he by Luciano's generosity.

"Gloria," Marco said after he took a moment, "it must be that Luciano feels guilt, and that he himself has to make up for the terrible actions of his son Andrea, since he is being so extraordinarily helpful with this reduced rent."

"Marco, it is not necessarily true that guilt is what has motivated Luciano!" Gloria advised him. "

We all have a pre-determined 'guidance system,' and the challenge is for us to be aligned with it. The Universe intended to give us what we want, and the feedback can be mysterious and unexpected. Marco, I believe that what Luciano did is beyond our old perception of him. What he just did was meant to be!

"Luciano always wanted to do good deeds, but he did not have a chance to do so before. Our activity with the Centers has attracted him to manifest his true desire—which is to help me. This provides him with the good emotions and feelings for which he yearns! His feelings also mirror our own joyous feelings.

"Remember the definition of the Law of Attraction: *That which is like, unto itself is drawn.'* Isn't it a joyful experience when two vibrations align together with the same thought and feeling? It is ironic that Andrea and I did not align together, but his father Luciano and I did."

Marco shook his head in wonder but kept on walking. He was taken aback by how quickly these new thoughts and paradigms were known to Gloria. Gloria's ability to learn so fast was astonishing!

For her twentieth birthday, Gloria enjoyed a small celebration that included immediate family only. Luca wanted a big party, but Gloria told him no.

As for Diana, she arranged for a cake for Gloria at the Center, so Gloria could celebrate with the girls as well. It was a happy moment for everybody, and the girls staying at the Center had prepared drawings and letters to express their affection for Gloria. As for Emma, she wrote a poem, one that truly impressed Gloria.

Deciding she wanted to enjoy lectures on the subjects in person, and to participate in class discussions, Gloria arranged with the Seminary to attend two classes in person one day a week. on

Not only did she wanted to dig into some topics more in-depth, Gloria also felt that it would be a healthy change to take a day off from the Center to focus on her own pursuits.

Wednesday was Gloria's day to go to Manhattan, and as he had in the past, Luca arranged for a driver to bring her there, and take her back.

On Gloria's first day, she found a seat next to a good-looking young man who looked like he was in his mid-twenties. The classroom was full of students working on their Masters or Doctorate degrees.

The topic for the day was about the convergence of New Science and New Spirituality. Gloria kept herself so busy taking notes, she was unable to ask the questions brewing in her head! So, at the end of class, she asked the man seated next to her a question about the lecture; he responded by asking her if she had few minutes to spare.

Gloria answered that she had a whole hour before her second class began, if only he could help her understand some of the material more deeply!

The two decided to go to the cafeteria nearby and have some coffee as they discussed what they had just learned in the lecture.

As they sat down in the cafeteria, the young man introduced himself. "My name is Peter Shepherd, and I have just finished my Master's. I am now working on my Doctorate degree in Divinity.'"

Gloria explained what she was doing at with her Centers, and Peter expressed his amazement that she had started such an undertaking at only twenty years old.

After Gloria asked her question and Peter helped increase her knowledge of the material they were studying, Peter told her that he was twenty-three years of age, and pondering the thought of becoming a pastor one day.

"What prompted you to consider this spiritual path?'"

"I come from a well-off family; my parents' main interest in life seems to be to make money and accumulate wealth. I felt that I was living in…a greedy and superficial world with them. My family only attracted people like them to socialize with, so for me, living there was an. empty experience. I was living a meaningless life, so I am trying to find a more meaningful way of living through my studies and learning. I live on my own in a small apartment in Manhattan now, although doing so infuriates my parents! They are pretty snobby, so they keep begging me to 'upgrade' my living quarters.'"

Gloria was quite taken by Peter's short story.

"I commend you on your clarity of mind, and your choice of how you want to live your life. I am blessed to have parents who approve of what I want to do with my life, and even though they are quite wealthy like your parents, they have become really supportive of my mission. I still live with them in a big house my father owns in the Bronx, and my Mercy Center is only ten minutes away. For a time though, as I figured out what to do in my own life, I lived in a convent to find my purpose.'"

"So you tried the convent life, and that is how you were able to decide to do this work of helping teenage girls? Is that your ultimate plan for your life, Gloria?"

"While I am aware of the direction I am heading towards," Gloria said thoughtfully, "my ultimate goal in life is not yet fully clear to me. It is.a work in progress. However, I am confident that the future will unfold and reveal unexpected wonderful events to me in due course.'"

The two new friends spoke for another thirty minutes and exchanged contact details before they went on to their other classes. They agreed to keep in touch, and Peter said he looked forward to seeing her next Wednesday.

As she arose from her chair, Gloria told Peter she appreciated the time with him and the wisdom he had shared, and invited him to visit her in the Center if he so wished.

She felt quite comfortable being around this young man who was charting his own future, one completely separate and detached from his family's advice and wealth.

In Gloria' second class about New Thought, she learned Christianity had evolved to introduce new concepts and doctrines based on love and positive thinking. This new diversity of thought, which had more focus on quality living instead of old rituals and non-practical guidance, was a magnet that attracted more and more followers, and brought continued growth, to New Thought churches.

Gloria was pleased to learn that the foundation for these new doctrines was solid, based on the teachings of Christ.

On Saturday of that same week, Peter called Gloria and asked her if he could come visit her at the Center. She told him she welcomed his visit, and Peter arrived approximately forty minutes later.

Gloria opened the door for him when he rang the bell. It was close to the lunch hour, and after they spent ten minutes talking together in her office, she invited him to join them for the lunch prepared by the girls staying with them.

She introduced Peter to everyone as her Seminary classmate, then asked the girls to each stand and state their names.

After they introduced themselves, Peter gave a small speech.

"Young ladies, I encourage each and every one of you to set goals for your life. I challenge you to believe that you are on this planet because each one of you had a purpose from the day you were born. All you need to do is to find out what it is, and then go for it!'"

The girls applauded his words before they continued eating their lunch.

After Gloria showed Peter around, Peter told Gloria how impressed he was with the work at the Center. He also told Gloria he admired her for her deep insight and love for people.

As the two drank a cup of coffee together in her office, Peter told her that he would like to assist the Center's mission through raising funds and donations. Gloria told him how much she appreciated this offer of help, and gave him the account number of her organization so that donations could be made.

Five minutes after Peter left, Diana walked into her office and with a facetious smile inquired, "So tell me, Gloria, are we looking at a potential relationship here?'"

"Come on, Diana, Peter and I only just met! He came here to tell me he wants to help us out by raising money for the Center. He comes from a very rich family, and he has many connections to rich people."'

"That is great of course, but do you *like* him?'"

"Diana," chided Gloria in an exasperated tone, "why are you pushing me about a relationship?! You should know I have no time for such things."'

"I like that the young man, Gloria, and I think the two of you will make a great couple. Open your eyes and see! He is not only great-looking, but he is also very spiritual—just your type. This man could be a rare find. You need to think about it."

"I appreciate your observation, and I will think about it,"Gloria laughed, "but can we go back to work now?'"

"Yes, okay," Diana chuckled. .

CHAPTER 8

A Wonderful Candidate

G loria was working at her desk when she received a call. The caller
identified himself as Jared, Emma's boyfriend.

Jared's voice sounded nervous when he said, "Miss Gloria, I have
been clean for the past four months, and I am determined to stay sober
for good. I value this new lifestyle, and I am doing better at work. I would
like to ask you if you would allow Emma to spend a weekend with me to
find out for herself how I have changed.'"

Gloria said, "I appreciate your call, Jared. I will think about it, and
call you back.'" "Thank you, and I eagerly await your reply," Jared said
before the call ended.

Gloria decided to double-check with the police if what Jared said
was true before she told Emma about his call. The officer she spoke
with told her that there were no reports of any relapses, and that Jared's
record was clean.

When it seemed appropriate, Gloria discussed Jared's request with
Emma.

Emma said to Gloria, "I would not mind spending this weekend with
him to find out for myself how he is living his life. Miss Gloria, I want you
to know I am not afraid of him anymore, so please do not worry about my
safety when I do."

Gloria nodded her head before she called Jared back and told him
Emma could spend that weekend with him starting on Saturday, and that
Emma needed to be back at the Center around six p.m. on Sunday.

Jared thanked Gloria profusely. He also promised to take good care of Emma, and to treat her with the respect she deserved.

Gloria continued to attend classes in the city on Wednesdays, and it had become a routine to spend her free hour before her second class talking with Peter.

Within three weeks' time Peter managed to raise a total of $65,000 for Gloria's organization from his parents and some of their friends. More than half this amount was pledged as repeating annual payments.

What drove Peter to raise funds for the Center was his belief in what Gloria was doing there, and his compassion. He was doing it simply to impress her because he liked her as more than a friend, although he did truly like her company. So one day during Gloria's free hour he asked her if he could visit with her at the Center every Saturday for a couple of hours around lunchtime for the foreseeable future.

With a smile, Gloria agreed to this new change in routine, and by the time the classes in the city were ending, the relationship between Peter and Gloria had grown into a strong friendship. They enjoyed each other's company, and often laughed together.

Gloria had never experienced such warm feelings towards anyone before. She continued to listen to her inner voice, and felt at peace with herself when it came to Peter. So the week before the official end of the semester, Gloria invited Peter to have coffee with her family.

Peter met Luca, Luisa, and Marco, and the visit with the Camino family was smooth and congenial. They all sat together in the living room, and Peter felt quite relaxed.

At one point Marco asked him if he likened his name to St. Peter. Peter chuckled and spouted off a few religious jokes about priests arguing with St. Peter in Heaven and how badly he needed a similar pass.

One of the jokes went like this:

> *A man dies and goes to heaven. St. Peter meets him at the pearly gates.*
>
> *St. Peter says, "Here's how it works. You need one hundred points to make it into heaven. You tell me all the good things you've done, and I give you a certain number of points for each item*

depending on how good it was. When you reach a hundred points, you get in."

"Okay," the man says, "I attended church every Sunday."

"That S good," says St. Peter, "that S worth two points."

"Two points?" he says. "Well, I gave ten percent of all my earnings to the church."

"Well, let's see," answers Peter, "that's worth another two points. Did you do anything else?"

"Two points? Golly. How about this: I started a soup kitchen in my city, and worked in a shelter for homeless veterans."

"Fantastic! That's certainly worth a point," he says.

"Hmm" the man says, "I was married to the same woman for fifty years and never cheated on her, even in my heart."

"That s wonderful," says St. Peter, "and that's worth three points!"

"THREE POINTS!!" the man cries. "At this rate the only way I get into heaven is by the grace of God!"

"Come on in!"

After the whole group laughed together, Gloria teased, "So all I get for my good deeds is one point for my soup kitchen?"

Peter answered, "No, Gloria, you get a full ten points right away. Your name is not Peter, and St. Peter likes to argue with men who carry his name!"

When coffee was over, Luisa told Peter he was welcome to come visit anytime he pleased in the future.

After Peter left, the family began peppering Gloria with questions about her new friend. They had r,had d as more than friend

Marco curiously asked, "Where and why have you been hiding this guy, little sister? He is so well mannered, funny, educated and good looking— well not as much as me, of course—but still, he is pretty great. And do you even know who this guy is? He hails from a family of Manhattan real estate tycoons!"

Before Gloria could respond, her father interjected, "Gloria, your friend seems to be a wonderful candidate in terms of someone about whom you can be serious. The two of you seem to have common interests, and both of you are motivated and inspired to live a spiritual life. It is not very easy to come across a man like him."

Gloria opened her mouth to reply, but her mother chimed in with, "Sweetheart, I am so happy to see you spending some time with a wonderful young man like Peter! You have been so serious since the episode with Andrea, and I started wondering if you will ever go out with a man. Please get to know him better...and try not to lose him! He seems like 'quite a catch,' if you don't me using that tired expression."

"Wow, can I talk now?" Gloria finally managed to say. "I appreciate what you all have just said, but I must beg you to take it easy on me! I admit I like the guy, but I am not rushing to commit myself to him or any other man before I clearly know what future is ahead for me.

"As for you, Marco, yes, I know who he is, but his family's wealth is not a factor in our relationship. I appreciate their donation to the Center, but Peter has no interest in their money or social status, and he doesn't like the lifestyle his parents live.

"Dad, I appreciate your comment on the common interests Peter and I share, and I still need more time to assess his approach to spirituality. I will nourish our friendship, and leave it to the Universe to guide us.

"And Mom, the fact I did not have any interest in men so far was due to my preoccupation with finding out whom I am first, and right now I am keeping quite busy doing the work I started. I am still young, as you all know, so don't worry about me and my romantic future, please. I am glad you all like Peter though, and maybe we could invite him to have dinner with us one evening so that you can get to know him even better.'"

Gloria's family nodded and began grinned upon hearing they might get an opportunity to see Peter again in the near future.

The first six months at the Center were coming to an end, and Gloria was pleased with the Center's achievements thus far. Fifty-four girls had been admitted during the six-months period, and all had been helped to some degree. Some stayed for as short as five days before being transferred to a professional service, whereas others stayed for fifteen days as they had different conditions that needed addressing or complicated circumstances to work out.

Of the fifty-four girls, twenty-two were pregnant, sixteen were emotionally disturbed or addicted to alcohol or other substances, and the rest had been abused either by members of their family or their boyfriends. Only ten of the twenty-two pregnant girls, whose average age was sixteen, knew who the father of their baby was. Fourteen of the pregnant girls ended up being placed in foster homes, and sixteen out of the twenty-two pregnant teens agreed to put their babies up for adoption.

The second Center was set to open in on month, and the organization already had more than $100,000 in its account, with donations pouring in on a regular basis. Emma was handling the books, and after a successful weekend visit with Jared, she told Gloria she desired to move back in with him while still continuing to work full-time during the week for the Center.

Gloria agreed to the new arrangement, with the provision that Emma start to accept a thousand dollars monthly for her work. She told Emma she wished it could be more, but she was trying to keep most of the dollars flowing to help fund the Centers' work. Emma was grateful for the salary, however small, and said she would have been willing to keep working without being paid because the Center had change the course of her life, including her relationship with Jared.

The new space for the second Mercy Center was ready to open and operate on time. The authorities and other affiliates had been notified about its grand opening, and Luca and the police chief had arranged for the Mayor to cut the ribbon with Gloria that day.

Member of the media also came to the event to cover the occasion. Luciano, Sister Delores and Mother Superior were present, and a reception with snacks and soft drinks was set for the sixty visitors that showed.

Later that same afternoon, the second Center received five new girls. This only filled the quarters partially, as the new Center could accommodate up to twenty girls at a time.

Gloria had asked Diana to be in charge of the new Center, and was giving her a decent salary for doing so. However, Gloria also planned to come visit the new Center every other day. Additionally, Luciano had found and arranged for two volunteers to help Diana, and the convent now was sending two Novices every day, one to each of the Centers.

As a result of the media coverage, there was a noticeable increase in monetary donations and number of people wanting to volunteer at the Centers.

Gloria was keeping quite busy with the running of both Centers, especially as she had one more year at the Seminary before she qualified for her degree in religious studies. She continued as an online student for most of her classes, while also arranging to attend classes two days a week in the city for the upcoming semester. She was willing to do this because her organization was in good hands, and she would have a chance to spend more time with Peter, who still had two more years to go before receiving his Doctorate in Divinity.

Despite wanting to spend a bit more time in Peter's company, Gloria was slow in developing romantic feelings for Peter… all that on; her life these days as busy and full!

Peter was much more comfortable expressing the way he was feeling about her. He told Gloria many times how he much he liked her, and that he was hoping that one day she would respond in kind. He said he was not expecting her to say she loved him yet, but merely hoped that she would express a desire to start dating and becoming more than just friends.

Gloria continued to immerse herself in analyzing the relationship between quantum physics and her own spiritual practice. She read that many were teaching that quantum physics was the new 'spiritual science.'

She noticed the teachers in this field referred to God as the 'Great Intelligence,' the 'Universe,' the 'Source of all Energy' or the 'Creator.' Very few referred to Him as Christians did— namely as,'God the Father,' or 'Jesus the Son of God' or the 'Holy Spirit.'

Gloria could not find in any of the 'spiritual' quantum physics books any reference to the Trinity, and she began to understand that many scientists believed in God, but not necessarily in the same way Christians did.

Gloria thought hard about the new shift in the terminology, and the beliefs that underscored the new schools of thought. She decided that she could not abandon her Christian faith and the teachings of Christ in particular—but neither could she refute the new beliefs and diversified teachings!

After much reflection, Gloria conclude that the ultimate goal of each school of thought and faith was the same. She wrote this in her journal:

Both sides—and even Eastern religion—have a common goal for the state of being of all people: They want people to live a life of love, happiness and peace.

I hope that I can be in a position one day to bridge the diinferences between these diiferent schools of thought and find a simple and common language that unifies them all. But I am still a novice in regards to my learning and understanding. I need to study these thought areas much more deeply over the upcoming years.

The next day after having written this, Gloria told Peter during their discussion time in the city about her desire to find a common language simple enough to explain a unified message of love, peace and joy to the world.

Peter sat silently for a while, and then said, "Religion is a very precarious field to study. Throughout history, and even before Christianity, religious beliefs have always been divisive, and also quite abundant in their differences from faith to faith.

"If you don't want to go too far back in time, look how the Christian faith has evolved. Nowadays you have dozens of different faiths within the Christian faith—and each one alleges to have the right answer to the human dilemma! Which one is easier to follow, and which one is not, thus becomes almost too impossible and complicated for people to figure out! That is why people choose one faith and abide by it until eventually it becomes a tradition they get used to.'"

"Yes, Peter, I hear you—that is exactly what I am talking about! How can we break the tradition of clinging to one faith because that's just easier, and instead, create one language that fits all? We have to get rid of all these labels— Catholics, Episcopals, Lutheran, Protestants and the like—not to mention the subdivisions within each. They are all Christians, for Pete's sake!?'"

At this point, Gloria let loose a giggle, and tossed an amused glance at Peter. "I don't mean you, Peter; sorry for my choice of words! To continue, if we cannot even unify all Christians under one school of thought, and teach them to use the same language and rituals, then how can we ever bring the other main religions, like Buddhism and Islam, to the table? I am afraid with all the religious divisiveness today, it is going to be much easier for people to eventually drop their religions completely, and identify themselves with the new phrase, 'I am only spiritual.'"'

"Gloria, I see you are being challenged to figure out how to safeguard your Christian beliefs, while also wanting to appreciate and adopt the validity of the new ones. I am afraid that will not be possible; in my mind, it has be an 'either or!'"'

"That is who I am, Peter, and I cannot shut my mind from such challenges as this! Many of us have surrendered to accepting—without even having a second thought about it—the old ways and practices with what we grew up. But if we go ahead and do this, we might miss out on many new ways and practice that could give us a better life!

"Peter, I saw this when I was at home with my mother. I saw it in the convent with the Sisters. I saw it in every church I visited. It has become redundant and boring. I would like to see a new paradigm by which all can all easily abide.'"

"Gloria, many great thinkers and religious leaders have tried to do this before you, and their success had been limited. I suggest you ease up on the search for an immediate answer. As I said earlier, religion is a very precarious field. Just focus on one thing at a time, and the rest will be revealed to you in due course.'"

"Well, it is easy for you to say!'"

As they walked towards their next class, Peter put his hand around her shoulder to help her relax a bit. He could tell that the lack of an answer in terms of a new paradigm was frustrating to Gloria. When she received the comfort of this embrace, Gloria turned around and hugged Peter in return.

It was the first time in over three months they had manifested their affection towards each other—and doing so felt good to both.

Before they parted after class, Peter told Gloria that he would like to introduce her to his family. He had not seen them in over a month, but he had told his mother about Gloria.

Gloria agreed to do that with him on Saturday evening.

Back home, Gloria told her mother about Saturday's planned visit, and asked her mother if she could go with her to buy some clothes suitable for the occasion. Luisa laughed, completely thrilled about the idea.

"Sweetheart, this is a good step forward! I would be delighted to take you to the best shop in Manhattan!'"

Gloria cautioned, "Mom, take it easy, please! The man is not proposing to me yet! It is just that I don't know these people, but from what Peter says I believe they might dress quite formally. I also want to look nice for them because I am grateful to them: They have helped the Centers financially, and they were responsible for raising Peter, who has become a close friend of mine.'"

"Well said, Gloria. I am glad to hear the word 'yet,'" Luisa teased, "and also that you two have become close friends. That will have to do for now! Let us go buy you some pretty clothes.'"

As the two shopped, Luisa confided in Gloria how everyone in the family has changed for the better, thanks to her.

When she heard this, Gloria asked her mother if she has experienced any change changed after reading the book she had given to her last Christmas.

Luisa paused for a moment, then said in a somewhat awkward tone, "I must confessed I have not read it yet! Sweetheart, I am satisfied and comfortable with my routine of attending mass every Sunday at my church. I enjoy being a member of that congregation, too!'"

Gloria nodded, but she did not say a word. She repeated to herself the saying, '*You can lead a horse to water, but you can t force it to drink,* 'and turned her attention back to the shopping.

Gloria ended up picking out two nice dresses and matching shoes. Her mother convinced her to buy other accessories, as well as facial creams and makeup. All these were new selections for Gloria, who had kept her look natural and clothing casual ever since she was a teen.

Luisa enjoyed treating Gloria to these things. She had always wished to dress Gloria up like this to showcase her physical beauty. She wanted Gloria to realize that while inner beauty is most important, there also is nothing wrong with a person enhancing their outer beauty.

They were back home before dinner, so Luisa asked Gloria to wear one of the outfits and put on some makeup to see how her brother and sister would react at the dining table.

Gloria walked down the stairs to join the family for dinner, and as soon as she walked into the dining room, there were loud cheers of appreciation. Her brother Marco whistled loudly, as if they were at a football game or something.

Gloria looked dazzling. They all told her how gorgeous she looked in her clothes, and Gloria assured them they had better not get used to this.

Marco started in on his sister, in his usual style. He teased, "So, my dear sister, did you decide on the 'big day' yet?'"

"Marco, stop being so presumptuous about my friendship with Peter! Why don't we pick on your girlfriend instead, and leave me alone!'"

"Actually, I don't have a girlfriend any more," Marco said quietly.

"Why, what happened?" Gloria asked, concern creeping into her voice.

"Well, if you actually want to know, she did not appreciate or accept my new way of thinking and the new choices I am making in my life. So it is not a real loss. I will not deviate from what I believe in now," Marco said decisively and with no trace of his usual humor.

"Well, as long as you feel good about it! And I am sure you will find the right partner soon.'"

"Now, seriously, how is it between you and Peter?'"

"It is good^very good, as a matter of fact. He is polite, intelligent, spiritual, and fun to be with. We hugged for the first time two days ago, and that is all we've done of a physical nature. He's invited me to meet his family this Saturday.'"

"Well, that is a good sign, my dear. Obviously the man really likes you, and I am glad you enjoy his company.'"

On Saturday, Gloria came home early to get ready for her trip to Manhattan. Luca arranged for a car and a driver to be with her.

The driver stopped the car in front of a stately old mansion on Fifth Avenue right across from Central Park. Gloria was a bit taken aback at the grandeur of the home and its slate roof, but she nonetheless exited her vehicle to go up and ring the doorbell.

A butler opened the ornate wooden door, and with a wave of his hand ushered her in. As Gloria stepped over the threshold, she saw Peter running down the winding staircase.

He came to an abrupt stop on the foyer's marble floor, looked her up and down and said, "Wow, is that you, Gloria? You look beautiful!'"

He welcomed her with a kiss on the cheek, then walked with her to the living room, where his parents were waiting.

Peter introduced her to his parents, Monica and Joseph Shepard. They stood up and greeted her with warmth.

Gloria was suddenly glad she dressed up. Peter's parents were well dressed, with his father in a dark suit and tie, and his mother in a long floral dress. Even Peter was wearing a dinner jacket!

Once they sat down at the mahogany dining room table, Peter explained to his parent what Gloria was doing to help and educate teenage girls in the Bronx, and that she had established two Centers.

Joseph Shepard, a dark-haired man with a hint of grey in his hair, reminded Peter they knew about the Centers already, for Peter had described them when he had asked for a donation

Then Monica asked Gloria, "I would enjoy hearing why you are choosing to spend your time in this manner when you are still so young and could be having quite a bit of fun doing other things!'"

Gloria said in a serene tone, "I was called to perform this duty. I had joined a convent for nine months to reflect on faith and religion, and that is when the idea came to me. There are many teenage pregnant women in the Bronx who are homeless and fleeing abuse, and I am happy to be able to provide a temporary shelter to them.'"

Joseph inquired, "Do you intend to be a nun for life, Gloria? Are you planning to return to life in the convent one day?'"

"No, I'm not, and I don't plan to go back. I chose to go reside in the convent for a maximum of one year to sort out some questions I had about the Christian religion and its influence on daily life.'"

The Shepards kept interrogating Gloria about her beliefs and plans for the future. She responded to all their questions briefly and in a humble manner, all the while not sure whether they understood and appreciated her reasons, or even if they were truly interested.

Twenty minutes later, dinner was served. At the table, the group talked about the changes taking place in Christian churches and how a shift to more modern practices has become more evident. Gloria realized was relaxed, and not intimidated by the fancy service and beauty of the mansion. Peter was the one who was silent the most, since his parents kept peppering Gloria with questions.

"Gloria, you have a long future ahead of you, so do you have an ultimate goal that you would like to achieve in your life?" Joseph asked.

"My purpose in life is to help others who are in need, spiritually, emotionally and physically. That is what really makes me happy. I believe that is the reason why I am here on this planet."

"Do you have a specific plan to achieve that?"

"In my opinion, the premise behind any plan is to ask in good faith and then surely it is given unto you. It starts with a thought that you put out in the Universe. If you believe in it with a burning desire, then the Universe—'God,' if you prefer—will give it to you in abundance and when it is least expected. The key word here is 'faith.' Believe in what you want, and trust you will get it."

"But Gloria, isn't it mainly hard work that we have to do to fulfill our dreams and goals?"

"Mr. Shepard, I am not underestimating the role of hard work in the process towards success. I *am* emphasizing and highlighting the power of faith and trust in what a person believes in and aspires to as being behind the necessary foundation underlying any of the hard work that follows.

"Faith is a power that is behind all great movements or great changes in the lives of human beings. Look at the spread of Christianity as an example!" Gloria declared, her voice rich with passion. "Faith was its basic foundation, and it continues to be despite all the reforms and evolution of Christianity's tenets. It all started with faith in what Jesus said and did.

"Look what Gandhi achieved by virtue of his faith in what he believed. The power of his faith transplanted peace into the minds of hundreds of millions of Indian people and gave them a better life. The same can be said about Nelson Mandela and how he changed the future of South Africa by ending the Apartheid regime. I could go on and on and mention many other great teachers or leaders who used their faith to empower their movements towards a positive change. But let me ask this instead:

Don't you agree, Mr. Shepard, that you achieved your success and fulfilled your dreams because you believed in what you wanted to do when you first started out? I believe you had strong faith within you, a burning desire that empowered you to bring about the results of your hard labor. You asked and you received. In your case, you attracted wealth, and the Universe responded and gave it to you.

"Now to go full circle and answer your earlier question about me, I know down deep in my mind and in my heart what I would like to achieve.

I am not there yet, but I am certain I am on the way. I focus on the 'now,' while I keep my vision for the future alive within me.

"Forgive me for such a long...dissertation! I would like to finish by saying that, like all the great leaders and teachers before us, I derive my satisfaction when I see other people benefiting from the fruits of my hard work."

There was silence around the table for few seconds before Joseph Shepard clapped his hands in admiration of what he had just heard. Peter was thrilled to see and hear his father's reaction to Gloria's words. Monica, Peter's mother, remained silent, but a smile of appreciation grew on her face.

The dinner finished with happy faces all around. The Shepards told Gloria she was welcome to visits any time she could, and as often as she might like. Gloria then left with Peter after giving warm hugs and thanks to her hosts.

Peter escorted her out to her car and told her how much he appreciated her visit. He kissed her goodbye on her cheek and walked back into the house feeling good about the depth of character Gloria had displayed—and his parents' reaction to it.

When Peter got back inside, his parents asked him to talk with them for a few more minutes. They settled in the spacious living room as his father began the conversation.

"I don't know what you think about her, Peter, but I must tell you this girl is a gem! I have yet to meet someone her age—and with her beauty, no less —to be so mature and focused about what really matters in life. Do you like her?'"

"Yes, very much, Dad and Mom. You know how reluctant I had been to go out with other girls before. I am not attracted to those of shallow character even if they have a high social status. Gloria is different, as you can see for your selves. She has an amazing brain in her head, and a huge heart in her chest. She thinks deeply and positively, and she has nothing but pure love for people in her heart.'"

Monica asked, "Do you two discuss have any plans for a future together?'"

"No, Mother, not yet. Yet we both know how we feel towards one another, and we both hold each other in great esteem. Don't forget we are still students and have other priorities at the moment.'"

"What other priorities?" Monica challenged her son. "Peter, this is a wonderful and unique young lady, and your top priority should be not to lose her. If the two of you love one another, then propose to her, and you can wait to get married later, perhaps when you graduate.'"

"Mother, take it easy, please!" Peter chuckled. "I am thrilled that you and Dad liked her, but she is only twenty, and I am sure that she is not ready to start a family yet. Actually, she is the one who has greater priorities and a busier life, and so I am certain she has a different timetable than all of us here.'"

"Peter, just remember you are the only son we have, and I would love to have Gloria as my daughter one day. May you both be guided to make the right decisions at the right time—and soon, I hope!'"

Joseph added, "Peter, I am really touched by what Gloria said, as that manifests the kind of person she is. She even has made me feel somewhat... guilty for not sharing a bigger part of my blessings to people in need. This woman has a unique power of influence and persuasion, and a great gift for clearly communicating her thoughts and ideas. Nourish this relationship as much as you can, and keep your eye and focus on her. I hope your mother and I can enjoy the two of you visiting us more frequently.'"

Peter thanked his parents for the wonderful evening, hugging them warmly before he left to go his humble abode.

CHAPTER 9

Traditional Religion & Modern Spirituality

Gloria was comfortable in the back seat of the car on her way back home. She took the time to reflect on her visit to Peter's parents. The following thoughts filled her mind:

It was an interesting evening, and I got to learn even more about me as well! I discovered I was relaxed, and not overly impressed by the show of wealth and the expensive surroundings. I was asked key questions, and I was forthright in my answers. I was able to clearly communicate what I wanted to say without any effort or stress.

I understand more now why Peter has chosen his humble life and a deefined spiritual path: He was not tempted by the huge fortune he is likely to inherit later through being the only son. He treated his parents respectfully tonight, yet remains loyal to his own choices in life. I liked his parents, who were inquisitive and keen to know who I truly am.

I am thrilled I was not bashful about dropping a small bombshell through my words to Joseph about helping others in need. All in all, it was a good evening, indeed!

Gloria rested well that night, and slept until nine a.m. Sunday. She later got ready to go to check on things at the second Center.

When Gloria arrived , Diana eagerly questioned her about Saturday evening at Peter's parents' house. Gloria told her briefly that everything had gone well, and that the atmosphere was jovial and pleasant. Diana wanted to hear more details, but Gloria told her there was nothing else to add.

The focus turned to operations at the new Center.

The second Center had been open for two months already, and its rooms occupied to full capacity. A total of thirty-five Gloria was kept busy there counseling those who needed emotional support and love.

As expected, the number of pregnant girls temporarily residing on the premises comprised more than fifty percent of the girls. These girls lacked the necessary knowledge so that they could care for and ensure the good health of their babies.

Another volunteer nurse had started helping out after the first week. She treated the girls who suffered from pain or other symptoms that sometimes came with those pregnancies not followed by a doctor.

The transferring of those to more professional facilities continued to go smoothly.

Emma was able to manage the books of both Centers, and she had become responsible for buying the required provisions for each Center, including the necessary food. eight o'clock until six o'clock, as she remained full of had done for In fact, h er life with Jared seemed to be working out; the young man was staying sober, and not experiencing any relapses. Emma also managed to get her GED through taking some online courses, and she got her degree with pride and joy.

There were seven people working in both centers now, including two daytime-shift volunteers and the two Sisters who visited from the convent. Centers' kept increasing, -So Gloria decided there were enough funds to be able to hire a full-time manager to oversee and manage the organization.

Gloria was searching for someone who was good in public relations and wh also had administrative experience. She put an ad out in the local papers, and also asked her friends and family if they knew of someone they could recommend. Within a week Gloria received seven resumes from different people who lived in the area.

The resumes that interested Gloria the most was from a man in his midthirties who had a Seminary degree that had qualified him to be ordained as a Pastor.

Father John had worked for six years as a pastor of a small church in South Bronx. The church was later closed, and that's when he became the head of a 120-member Christian youth group organization registered in the Bronx. Gloria quickly called for an interview.

Father John arrived to meet Gloria in her office at the first Center the very next day. She started the interview by asking him, "What do you know about us, and what we do?"'

"First, your work is well-known in the area now. I watched the media coverage of the opening of the second Center, as your organization is of interest to all of us who are involved in doing good deeds for others. Second, I learned from friends in the local government about who you are and the unique vision you have had to help out some of the local teenage girls."'

"Father, why are you interested in not continuing your fine work in the youth group organization? I know about what you do there as well!"'

"The organization's new budget provided by the higher Church authorities interferes with me managing the group adequately. I am running out of the funds required to keep all the activities going as planned. The monies are so insufficient, I am afraid they are planning to close our chapter of the organization. I prefer not to see that happen, as the membership is comprised of young and promising kids."'

"What salary would you need to do the job described in the ad I put out?"'

"I live in a small one-bedroom apartment, and I was able to manage that and my other expenses with being paid $2,000 a month in salary. I think I could manage with the same kind of earnings from your organization."'

"That sounds reasonable, as we are adequately funded by donors and generous gifts. We have two Centers now, and we might establish a couple more in due course. Seven people currently work in these centers, including some volunteers and help from the convent. However, the growth of our work is such that we need an administrative manager for the organization who is also capable to coordinate the flow of our guests to the right groups we cooperate with for their long-term care or issues. How do you think you might be able to help us out here?"'

"I imagine that, by now, you have a large budget to feed and take care of the girls. Well, I have ample experience in managing budgets and keeping expenses low. In fact, I am able to buy provisions from suppliers who give me a special rate. There are even some I know who are willing to supply food free of charge if we can accept leftovers from the previous day. I did all of that in my current organization, and I know what to choose and whom to work with. Morever, almost everybody in the local police department knows me well, and I imagine you receive some of the girls who stay in your facilities from their dealings with the police.

"I also have dealt with hospitals and clinics on several occasions to take care of some young people who needed care that they could not afford, and those connections might prove helpful in terms of any pregnant teenagers living here, or for those young people who may have other health issues. I can teach the young about the love of God, and how to live a good quality life away from the street.'"

"Father John, those qualifications are perfect for the position! When would you be able to start, and would you always be wearing your black outfit with the while collar?'"

"I can start in two weeks, after I give my official notice to my current organization. And yes, I plan to keep wearing the same attire; I find it opens up many doors for me.'"

"That's good to hear. So we have a deal, and when you are ready, I will walk you through the Centers and introduce you to the staff.'"

"Thank you, Miss Gloria. I am free this afternoon if you are.'"

"Father John, please call me Gloria.'"

That afternoon Gloria escorted Father John around the first Center. She showed him the downstairs area first, introducing him to the staff. She then took him upstairs to see the dormitory where the girls slept.

After she finished the tour, she called Diana to tell her that she was hiring Father John, and to be ready to receive him when he arrived in fifteen minutes.

Father John thanked Gloria and took a taxi to the second Center to meet Diana. Diana walked him about the space, and he had time to even talk to some of the girls living there.

After, Diana called Gloria to say that she thought Father John was a great choice to manage the organization.

Gloria saw Peter after class the first day of the week. He told her how much his parents had appreciated her visit and her conversations with them. Peter then said, "They would like us to visit with them more frequently, Gloria.'"

"What type of pressure does that put on you, Peter? I know you don't approve of their lifestyle.'"

"No, I do not, but I'm fine with it as long as we visit them together. Having you present with me makes it easier for me to be more tolerant of their way of life.'"

"Am I a crutch for you to lean on?" Gloria teased.

"No," Peter chuckled, "but if I may be candid, they would like to see us together all the time. Tand —, "So they are putting pressure on you in that sense," Gloria said, giving an affirming nod of her head. "How are you going to handle that?'"

"Well, Gloria, it really is not up to them to decide our destiny, is it? We are mature people who can decide on our own. I know I like you, and I hope you like me in the same way, but this does not mean we are ready to make further commitments in our relationship beyond friendship. I have told my parents that, and I do hope they understood, but the thing is, they loved you so much, they would like to see us become a couple. My father called you a 'rare gem,' and my mother called you, 'unique.' So now you understand why they want us to visit them more frequently!'"

"You did right, Peter, to tell them we are not ready for any more commitments now. We both believe in the power of God, and we leave it to Him to guide us if and when it becomes His wish to see us together.'"

Gloria went back to the second Center the same afternoon and met with Diana. She spoke again to Gloria about how impressed she was with Father John, and told her she had spent enough time with him to undertsand why he was so popular with the young people.

She also confided that Father John had told her that he was a bit intimidated by Gloria, since she was in charge of such an operation at such a young age. Diana said she had put him at ease in this regard, telling him that Gloria was a wonderfully approachable young woman.

Diana then told Gloria that it might be a good idea for Father John to have his office in the second Center, since the space there is much larger than in the first Center.

Gloria smiled upon hearing this, for she sensed that Diana, who had recently turned twenty-five, might be somewhat attracted to Father John. Gloria gave Diana the go-ahead to coordinate the work on Father John's office with their architect.

Two weeks later Father John joined the Mercy Centers. His office was located in the front section of the space at the second Center, not far from Diana's office.

The first task he did was review the expenses the organization usually paid for food and other sundry supplies. He managed to negotiate these down by about twenty percent within a week's time. He also arranged to have medical robes, gloves, syringes and the like supplied for free from nearby hospitals.

Father John then spoke with Diana about establishing more disciplined daily schedules for the girls to follow, and the benefits that would accrue from this change.

Diana was delighted to have him around, and the two of them got along well.

Gloria and Peter took a course together about Modern Spirituality. After class one day they decided to discuss the subject while having coffee at the cafeteria.

"Peter, you are ahead of me in your knowledge about religious studies and perhaps the concept of modern spirituality. Can you explain to me how modern spirituality has evolved?'"

"In my previous studies I always understood spirituality as a religious form of expression. So modern spirituality is actually a new study for me, just as it is also new to you," Peter confessed.

"For me, Peter, spirituality is when I choose the concept of love as the purpose of my life, and I believe that is all what really matters. So I must say I am somewhat confused by the lecture we just heard. Spirituality has become so much more diversified, with so many different definitions and practices.'"

"That is true, Gloria, and it has become in vogue nowadays. As we heard, 24 percent of the American population now identify themselves as, 'spiritual but not religious.' This is happening because these converts want to find their own spiritual path to connect with God or the Universe; they don't want to follow the popular path of old religious teachings.'"

"Yes, so I heard. But I thought that spirituality is a process that recovers the relationship between man and God. I also realize spirituality differs from one religious practice to the other, meaning in Christianity it is attained via Christ, in Buddhism via Buddha, in Islam via Mohammad, and in

Judaism via the Torah. However, nowadays it has become more personal and subjective, often totally separate from that found in organized religions.'"

"The professor also said that modern spirituality is a blend of humanistic psychology and mystical traditions of Eastern religions. Some of today's spiritual practices are even secular, in that they are simply practiced to help resolve mental health issues, marital concerns, and the like.'"

"I was alarmed to hear, Peter, that since the 20th century there has been a distinction between religion and spirituality due to the rise in secularism and the start of the New Age movement. Many people are targeting self-realization via free expression and meditation.'"

"What is really worth noticing, though, is the fact that there is added interest in incorporating 'spiritual care' as a component to complement health care. Many new studies are showing that religious or spiritual people tend to be in better health! This knowledge that spirituality can protect against illness is bringing science and religion closer together.'"

"All that is good, but a big disconnect has taken place from the original development of early Christianity, where life was oriented toward the Holy Spirit, to the current wide range of spiritual experiences that include Eastern traditions.'"

At this point Gloria looked at Peter with a concerned and questioning look on her face.

"Gloria, don't forget about those new findings by neuroscientists that spiritual experiences in specific areas of the brain can be easily awakened by meditation or other transcendent practices.'"

Gloria thought for a second before she said, "In brief, Peter, the advent of spirituality and its distinction from religion has impacted the growth of organized religions and opened the door to so many different shades of 'spiritual schools of thought.' I find this challenging to accept, and I would like to figure out a method that would halt the decline in church membership and attendance. Perhaps I could come up with modern spiritual concepts that complement traditional religious practices?'"

"You plan to take it upon your shoulders to bring about such a change?'" he asked, visibly startled.

"Yes, why not?" Gloria answered in a confident tone.

Peter was astounded to hear that reply and thought to himself, *My friend here is definitely unique, and has very little interest in living a conventional life! I had better be prepared for such an eventuality, as it is could be quite demanding to be with such a great thinker and achiever like Gloria is.*

As if Gloria read his mind, she inquired, "What are you thinking about now, Peter?'"

With complete sincerity Peter said, "Well, that I find you quite unique! You, my dear friend, are someone who sets a very high standard for her life!'"

Gloria gave an agreeable c laugh, then got up to go about her business for the rest of the day.

Peter too rose to his feet, but he stopped her from leaving right away by asking, "Gloria, is it possible for us to see each other one evening, and not only between classes or for lunch on Saturdays? I know you are very busy, but I really would like to see you more frequently.'"

"Why don't you come up this Saturday afternoon to the Center, and from there we go on to have an early dinner at an Italian restaurant I know in the Bronx?"

"It's a deal. I will see you in your office at four o'clock this Saturday,'" Peter promised, a smile racing over his face.

On Saturday morning Gloria called Father John to her office and said, "I do hope you are enjoying your new job, and I appreciate what you have done already. Diana briefed me on all the wonderful changes you have implemented already.

"I wanted to ask you if you feel equipped to organize a one-day conference sometime in the next two to three months. It should consist of three sessions, with two lectures with questions and answers in the morning, and one in the afternoon.

"There will be a one-hour lunch break, and thirty minutes for tea and cookies between the two morning lectures. We will offer attendance, meals and refreshments free of charge. many, so I have chosen the subject to be, 'Sexuality in Christianity.' have to we desire What do you think about such an event?'"

"Gloria, it's a great idea! I am very comfortable organizing these kinds of events, for I have done quite a few of them in the last five years. If you are focusing on the Bronx borough, then the venue should be around here. I know of a nice, clean hotel not far away that has a good size ballroom that can easily accommodate three hundred people. The hotel's staff knows me, and I arrange for a special deal with them for the ballroom space, food and drinks.

"I also know a local publicist who can prepare brochures to send out, and ads to place in the local papers. I can also arrange for an ad in one local religious channel for free. Let me start working on this, and I will get back to you with more details, including the speakers we should invite.'"

Peter arrived at four p.m. that afternoon. He waited for Gloria in her office as she was still counseling one of the girls in the conference room. Diana brought Peter some tea and cookies, then she introduced him to Father John, who happened to be walking by. The two men were able to talk for about ten minutes before Gloria returned to her office. Once Father John left, Diana and Peter started a conversation together, with Gloria bringing up what was currently on her mind.

"It's good to see you again, Peter! I recently hired Father John to run the organization's administration and its public relations. This morning I told him I wanted to set up a one-day conference soon to talk about sexuality in Christianity. Did he tell you anything?'"

"No he didn't," Peter answered after choking on a sip of tea, "but what a topic you have chosen! You are very courageous indeed.'"

"Well, look at what we do here: More than half our cases are pregnant teenagers who come from a poor background and have very little education. It doesn't make any sense to keep our mouths shut; we have to address the issue publically.'"

"You chose a very controversial subject for the conference, and it will arouse some criticism from different those who hold different viewpoints," he said, giving Gloria a bit of an apprehensive look.

"That is fine with me, Peter. I don't mind a certain level of...provocation, shall we say, arising as a result of holding an event on this topic. Unless we address pertinent issues such as this, we will not be able to improve the quality of life for these young people! I am only inviting teenage boys and girls to attend; well, maybe their parents too, although I am not sure yet. We need to educate them about the havoc generated from untimely sexual behavior.'"

"I agree with that last statement, Gloria, but what I am trying to understand is why this theme for the conference: Most ears out there prefer not to hear these two words joined together. They know already that Christianity is strict about anyone having premarital sex, and they don't want to talk about it. Christian leaders avoid addressing the problem, even though they know it exists, and the church leadership may reprimand you for bringing this subject out in the open. They prefer to hide their heads in the sand and pretend they do not see what is going on in society.'"

"Are you telling me I should change the theme and the title of the event? Do you think I should be like them and hide from the topic?" Gloria asked Peter assertively, her cheeks flushing with anger.

"Relax, Gloria; you don't have to be so aggressive or highly opinionated! Forgive me for saying so, but is okay to be flexible and diplomatic on occasion. You need to allow yourself some time before you reach the stage where you do not care about what others think. Gloria, your work and you fame will grow step by step, piece by piece. You are not there yet, and you cannot turn your back on the Christian leadership yet. Slowly you will win their hearts and be quite able to do what you want. Let us find some terminology that replaces the use of 'Christianity.' Perhaps you call the theme, 'Sexual Immorality' or 'Sexual Morality' instead."

"Well, it's true I am not a conformist, and I believe in change. But I appreciate your comments and observations, and I need time to think about them," Gloria said in a calmer manner. "I guess I did may have sounded a bit aggressive."

"Thank you. Please know that in general, I agree with the concept of educating and alerting the community through this type of a conference, which I am certain will attract the attention of many young people. We just need to tread a bit more carefully. Are still on for our Italian dinner this evening?"

"Of course! Just give me thirty minutes to finish up here. Go talk to the girls sitting around; they would love to chat and flirt with you," she joked.

Peter and Gloria walked for about seven minutes to reach the Italian restaurant Gloria chose. She told Peter her father liked this place a lot, and he used to bring the family to eat there frequently.

The restaurant owner recognized Gloria the moment she walked in, and he gave the couple a nice quiet table by the window. Then he poured each of them a glass of his favorite red wine from Sicily.

After they reviewed the menu and ordered their dishes, Gloria said, "That was quite a discussion we just had in my office. Do you truly think I am beings .overly presumptuous?"

"Not exactly. You are just too...excited about your work and your mission in life, and that makes you rush to get your plans done at a faster pace than what is customary and necessary."

"Boy, Peter, you would make a great diplomat!" Gloria observed as she took a long sip of wine. "That is good, so clearly I have a lot to learn from you. I agree with what you are saying, and I actually don't always understand why I am always in such a hurry. I do need to relax a bit, and learn that I do need to do ten things at the same time."

"Gloria, am I adding to the load you are carrying?" Peter asked curiously. "By asking you to increase the amount of time we spend together?"

"Peter, don't be silly! I love spending time with you, and I do want to see you more often. Your being by my side helps me to realize that there are other important aspects to my life I should not ignore. Our friendship during the last four months has been delightful and reassuring. I feel good when I see you, and I am attracted to your character, your thought process, your attitude about life, and of course, your fantastic looks."

"Thank you, Gloria, I am so flattered to hear these remarks from you. I thought that you don't care about such feelings; clearly, I was wrong. This encourages me to tell you how much I admire you. In fact, I think the world of you. You are multi-gifted, blessed with the greatest mind and heart anyone could hope to find, but also very beautiful on the outside. I consider it something of a reward just to know you."

"Thank you, Peter, for sharing how you feel towards me too. I realize we are both still young and students, but I am wondering whether you are satisfied with where we are now in this relationship, or do you have other aspirations?"

"If you are talking about a long-term commitment, the truth is that I do want to see us together forever," Peter said, his eyes aglow for a moment. "That being said, I also realize it is best for us to be patient for another year or so until I graduate before we can address a plan for our continued togetherness as a couple.'"

"Peter, you should be a writer or a famous speaker soon! You know how to say something without really saying it, especially through the wording of, 'Before we can address a plan for our continued togetherness as couple.'""

"Gloria, what do you mean? Do I need to rephrase this sentence? Do you not understand the intention behind it?'"

"No, no, understood it very well," Gloria clarified. I just like the way you choose your words. Others would have said, 'Before I can propose to you.'"

"Well," Peter admitted, a blush suffusing his cheeks, "I prefer more of a soft landing instead of a sudden and unexpected fall!'"

"Peter, I agree with you that it is not time yet to climb that...high. We will continue to nourish this relationship with patience and respect for each other, and the Universe will definitely guide us to the right time and the right decision.'"

'I agree, and Gloria? I am not going anywhere. God bless us both, and we will see what the future holds in store for us.'"

As the two began to eat, Gloria unexpectedly spied Marco walking into the restaurant with a young beautiful girl. She gave a wave to her brother, and he came over to say hello.

"Gloria and Peter, wonderful to see you tonight! I did not know you would be here! I'd like to introduce my friend, Lula.'"

Peter and Gloria gave a warm hello to the slim brunette, who greeted Peter and Gloria with a sincere smile. Then Marco then accompanied his new friend to sit at the table reserved for them at the other side of the restaurant.

Gloria took another bite of her ravioli before asking in her typical blunt fashion, "Peter, are you comfortable that you and I cannot have sex together yet?'"

Peter's eyes flew open wide, and he shook his head in bemusement. "My goodness, Gloria, you always are a 'straight shooter! What prompted you to say that?" But without waiting for an answer, Peter continued, "To answer your question, yes, I am. The other aspects of the relationship that exist between us are far more rewarding at this stage than physical pleasure. I am patient and I can wait. Not for too long though, I hope!'"

"What do you mean? How much longer can you wait?'"

"As long as it takes until you give me the first signal!'"

"You mean the signal to get married first, before we sleep together?'" Gloria asked to clarify.

"Yes, your excellency, yes! We are both devout Catholics, and I know both of us believe in the sanctity of marriage.'"

"Fine, then. Now I know that you can wait patiently for another five to ten years. That is wonderful!" Gloria said with enthusiasm.

Peter's eyes once again opened wide until he realized she was joking.

After Gloria stopped her giggling, she said with a renewed seriousness in her tone, "Peter, I will be twenty-one soon, and I will finish my degree in about one year. You will finish your doctorate in less than two years. By then I will be twenty-two and you will be twenty-five or twenty-six by then. That will be a good time for us to consider sharing vows if we are still interested. Meanwhile, we will continue to grow in our knowledge, our work and our feelings toward one another. Is that schedule okay?'"

"Yes. That sounds good to me.'"

As the two finished up their entrees, Marco came over and asked them to enjoy some dessert at the table he shared with Lula. Gloria and Peter readily agreed, and they joined Marco and his date. Soon enough, the owner brought them all his homemade *tira misu.*

Gloria spoke in a low tone over the dessert with Lula, while Marco spoke to Peter.

Gloria discovered Lula had met Marco at a half-day seminar given by the authors Esther and Jerry Hicks, who had written bestselling books based on the Universal Law of Attraction. Since Marco had become obsessed with the Universal Law of Attraction over the last year, and Lula tried to live by it in her life, the two had had a lot in common. They also had discovered it was quite easy for the two of them to converse with one another.

Thirty minutes later, they all left the restaurant. Peter hailed a taxi to take him back to his place in Manhattan since Marco had offered Gloria a ride home in his car with him and Lula.

After he dropped Lula off at her place, Marco asked Gloria what she thought of Lula.

"Marco, I quite like her, although we did only have a short time to speak. She seems since and authentic. However, what matters most is how you feel about her. What do you think of her since meeting her at the seminar?'"

"I like Lula a lot, and especially because of her desire to live a similar spiritual life to mine! I have only known Lula for two weeks, but I hope the relationship will continue to move in the right direction.'"

"I hope so too, Marco. As for me, Peter and I are doing well, and as of tonight we are beginning to talk about the possibility of a future spent together."'

Marco grinned when he hear this. He liked Peter very much, and thought he would be a supportive spiritual and romantic partner for his sister Gloria.

CHAPTER 10

Giving the Message

A pproximately a week after Gloria surprised him with the news of a conference, Father John told Gloria he had booked a hotel where the conference could be held. He gave her the dates, as well as details of the deal he had struck with the hotel.

He also advised her he had met with a publicist, who was ready to prepare brochures, mailing lists, and ads to put in the local paper. Father John added that the religious TV channel he had contacts at was willing to broadcast a fifteen-minute video from the conference on their channel.

"Good job, Father! It appears all is set, except we still need to book speakers for it! By the way, I have been deliberating about the topic of the conference. Some concerns were raised about the wording of the theme, and I have decided to change the name of the conference to, 'Sexual Immorality.'"

"Okay, so noted. As regards the speakers, I recommend that we ask Father Michael, whom I know very well from when I was a student at the Seminary with me. He is currently the spiritual advisor to the City Mayor. He is well versed on the subject at hand, and may even encourage the Mayor to attend his speech."

"That is a good idea, Father John, and maybe we should make him the keynote speaker in the afternoon! As for the Mayor, his presence would attract many people to attend as well, so let's hope Father Michael recommends our conference to him."

"May I also suggest that you be the first speaker in the morning session?" Father John said unexpectedly.

"Me? Are you kidding? Why would those who come want to hear from me?'"

"You are the sponsor of the event, and you are passionate about the subject at hand. You have great communication skills, and you have no stage fright.'"

"You don't think it will appear as a self-serving attempt to promote the work I do through the Centers?'"

"So what if it does? Let people know who you are, and you shouldn't be shy about the great work you are doing, and why. It will predominantly be a young audience at the conference, and my opinion is no one would be better to get the message across to them than you, who also happens to be another young person.'"

"You are a very good salesman, Father!" Gloria teased. "Are you sure you have the right job here?'"

"I am very happy here," Father John said with complete sincerity, "and I know a lot about how young people think and behave. Trust me, you can do it —*and* it will be the best speech ever. You will see.'"

"Fine," Gloria capitulated. "We do still need a third speaker, and I am wondering whether we can find someone who is not a religious man or women, but an expert who has written books on the subject of teenage pregnancies.'"

"Well, we may be able to draw some speakers from the Religious Institute in Bridgeport, Connecticut. I am sure they who would love to send a member of their staff to speak about any subject, even sexuality, to an event like the one we are planning.'"

"Perhaps in the future, Father John; for now, I really would prefer a famous expert who has written a book on this subject. He or she does not have to be a religious practitioner. In fact, it would be even more ideal if it is some medical doctor with a spiritual background.'"

"You mean someone like Dr. Deepak Chopra? An M.D. turned into a spiritual teacher?'"

"Absolutely! Someone like that will be a dream come true!" Gloria said, her eyes alight with possibility.

"I will do some research and get back to you with some suggestions."

The meeting ended with Gloria thinking about the idea to give a speech on the subject as suggested by Father John. She thought, *Well, is not such a bad idea! It will help to establish my position as a leader in this community, and f I can do that, many might listen to me and support my future plans for spiritual solutions to bigger socioeconomic and health issues. I have a vision for my future that is much larger than the work I am doing at the present moment, so I should take this opportunity and make it my own.*

One day I desire to receive a guided message based on the teachings of all great spiritual teachers, although primarily Jesus Christ. I want it to appeal to people of all religions and sects, so I need to deepen my knowledge on all such great sources of information, including engaging in a deeper study of the Bible.

Right now I have access to, and references for, several books from the courses am studying. I can and should refer to these books to enlighten my mind. Then, and most importantly, I wait for a divine signal to lead me on the right path.

Perhaps Peter, with his increased education in the spiritual realm can be of help also.

Gloria met with Peter later on in the day at the Seminary's garden. The two sat on a small wooden bench as Gloria shared her discussion with Father John, and the unexpected request that she give the opening speech. She also shared with Peter her thoughts about her future plans for a 'message' to the world. Gloria then looked at Peter and asked for his opinion.

"So Peter, what do you think? Should I give a speech at the conference?'"

"It is a normal practice in conferences like this for the organizer, and founder of the organization to give a welcoming speech that explains the purpose of, and the inspiration behind, the conference's theme.'"

"I have never written something like this before. Will you help me with the speech?'"

"You are a very smart woman, so it is best for you to write it yourself, but I can help edit it for you. Put all your thoughts down and I will touch it up with my out-of-this world style!" he laughed.

"That sounds good, my professor! We will work on it together then. I have another question, and it's regarding the message that we talked about recently, the one that I keep dreaming about. Any input or enlightening ideas from you in regards to it?'"

"Sweetheart, it is your vision and your dream. When it becomes clearer in your head, share it with me and we will work together on how to structure it and write it down. But you are the one who has to be inspired and guided first.'"

"I don't know how soon I will be guided with the right message. Is it all right if it takes me a couple of years still?'"

"It will be my pleasure to wait until you are ready," Peter assured her, "and I look forward to many joint projects together with you in the future. Your inspired and unique thoughts are exciting, and are part of what attracts me to you."

Gloria was pleased to hear him say this. The two stood up feeling good, and they held hands as they proceeded to their class.

A week later Gloria met with Father John for an update on the conference, as it would be taking place in only five weeks. He walked into her office smiling and said in an excited voice, "I have found a doctor who works at the Bronx Medical Center—with which the Centers are associated—and who has treated several of our own girls there. She is Dr. Francesca Albright, a Christian pastor who got her M.D. six years ago and now supervises the OB-GYN department at the hospital. She is willing to help us. She has treated a couple hundred teenage pregnancy cases already, and she highly appreciates what we are doing in our Centers. I highly recommend her, Gloria. She meets the qualification in that she is both a medical doctor and a spiritual being. In addition, she is from our area, and that should resonate well with the audience. What do you think?'"

"That sounds great, Father! Can you arrange for us to meet? Either I can go to see her or she can come to see me; whatever is most convenient for her.'"

"I will ask her and let you know. By the way, Father Michael will be speaking at our event, and he is waiting to hear from the Mayor about whether he can attend. So now we have the three speakers lined up, including you of course.'"

Gloria pointed her index finger at him with a smile and said, "You^ you are good you.'"

Father John smiled upon hearing the popular phrase Gloria had quoted from the movie, 'Analyze This,' then left to conduct more successful business for the Centers.

That afternoon Gloria went to visit the second Center. Diana met Gloria there, and reported that all was going well. All of the rooms were occupied, and apart from minor pains that some of the pregnant girls had experienced, no other concerning incidents had occurred.

Diana then spoke with Gloria how happy she was to have Father John managing the Centers.

"Father John was a great hire, Gloria! Not only has he saved the Centers quite a bit of money in terms of buying our provisions, but the girls really appreciate his guidance and the programs he's scheduled for each day.'"

"How are the two of you getting along each day?" Gloria asked curiously.

"Funny you should ask! Actually, we get along really well. We both feel a certain level of...warmth between us that we are keeping an eye on.'"

"Care to elaborate on that, Diana? I am your friend!" Gloria reminded her with a smile full of affection.

"As you may remember, the original reason I went to the Convent was to cleanse my soul from an emotional setback I had with another man. Since then I have taken an oath of abstinence not to be with another man until marriage. I discussed that decision with Father John, and he said he has taken the same oath for himself. If you didn't realize, he is not Catholic, so he can marry one day if he chooses. He plans to wait until the right person comes. So."

At this point Diana's voice trailed off. Gloria looked at her for a moment before prompting, "So *what* exactly, Diana? Are you considering getting married to each other one day in the future?'"

"Maybe!" was Diana's surprising response. "The idea is still fresh in our minds, and there are other things to consider before we take such a step.'"

"Such as?'"

"Well, who is going to be responsible to stay with the girls here day and night? If we are married, we will have to live together, no?'"

"Diana, my dear, that is a minor issue," Gloria counseled, "and we can always find the right person to stay with the girls 24/7 at the Center in due course. What matters are the affairs of your heart and what sounds like a future together with Father John; that is what you need to focus on.'"

"Thank you, sweet Gloria," Diana beamed, "and I will keep you apprised! Meanwhile, since we are on the subject of romance, may I ask you about your relationship with Peter?'"

"All is well. We both like one another a lot, but we are 'taking it easy' as far as being together under the same roof. I am too young, and he still has another year to go to finish his doctorate. If the relationship remains on this path, I see us getting married one day too. You will be the first to know, curious Diana.'"

"Thank you for the update. Who knows; maybe we can get married at the same time!" Diana laughed.

Gloria arched an eyebrow, then simply said, "Enjoy the rest of the day, Diana! It is always so good to see you. I will walk around and say hi to the girls and volunteers before I leave.'"

Gloria greeted everybody at the Center, then thanked her helpers. She stopped to spend a few extra moments with Emma, who reassured that all was well at home: Jared was still sober and in recovery, and also steadily working at a job. Emma also told her that the donations seemed to keep coming in on a regular basis, and they currently have eight months in reserve for running the Centers.

Later that day, Gloria was enjoying dinner with her family. Marco was there alone, not with his new girlfriend Lula. This gave Marco an opportunity to tell Gloria how satisfied he is in his new relationship.

According to Marco, Lula continued to impress him with her spiritual growth. He said that she recently taught him a short ten-minute guided morning meditation by Abraham Hicks.

"Gloria, the focus is on raising our vibration level by being in touch with our inner being, and remembering that every new day is a good day. The purpose of the morning meditation is to align our being with the Source, or God. It is like a modern prayer of sorts.'"

This last sentence caught Luca's attention.

"What do you mean by, 'a modern prayer,' Marco?'"

"Well, Father, the teacher of this meditation is not your...typical kind of religious person who teaches prayers similar to what we learned in school or in church. Nevertheless, she is spiritual. She channels the voice of a God-like 'spirit' when she speaks, and it is very positive. She holds seminars and gives speeches during which she answers all kinds of questions from her audience. Her message appeals to millions of people around the world.'"

"Are you saying that most people—people today—don't go to church or pray as they used to?" Luisa challenged.

"Yes, you could say that, Mom, and it's unfortunate. This trend—really, it's a new movement—was caused mainly by the failure of Christian leaders to adapt the Church's teachings to the contemporary needs of people. Traditional religion has been losing its 'luster' for decades now in terms of attracting and keeping followers, and there are not serious efforts by the leadership to implement noticeable changes that might attract people back into its fold.'"

"So the Church is being old-fashioned and out of touch, in other words,'" Luca observed in a tense tone, clearly not happy to hear Marco's comments.

Gloria interrupted this conversation to ask Marco, "Isn't Abraham Hicks the expert on the Law of Attraction? I remember you and Lula had mentioned this to me earlier.'"

"Yes. The whole thing was started by Esther Hicks and her husband Jerry many decades ago. They were connected with that movie, 'The Secret' that I told you about earlier. In the last couple of decades, Abraham, who is the guiding spirit of Esther, has channeled his answers through her with blocks of thoughts of collective consciousness to the questions asked by anybody.'"

"I really should read those books," Gloria noted. "I am eager to learn more about her, but I must admit, I've had trouble finding the time with all the readings I am currently doing for my Seminary courses.'"

Luisa asked in a tone full of dismay, "So now you two are more interested in this attraction/vibration thing? You are no longer interested in our Catholic teachings, the teachings with I raised you on?'"

"No, Mother, and actually, quite to the contrary!" Marco observed. "These modern new teachings enhance people's relationship with God, the Source of all energy, and importantly, they complement the teachings of Jesus Christ! The only thing is that this new form of spirituality—along with many other forms—does not support traditional organized religion, and the unjustified power the Church has had over its people for years.'"

"Well, it sounds quite...wrong to view the Church in that way!" Luisa said, clearly upset. "I am surprised at you, Marco! I am sticking to my old faith, and no one will stop me from going to church every Sunday. Isn't that so, Luca?" Luisa said emphatically.

"Um, I guess so, Luisa! All this stuff is Greek to me, anyhow," Luca answered half-heartedly, trying to make a joke of it...

Those at the dinner table got up then to go their separate ways for the evening. As for Gloria, she told Marco in a hushed tone she wanted to have a private discussion with him on the subject very soon.

Gloria left the dinner table wondering, like her mother Luisa, how her brother had so quickly become such a big fan of the Law of Attraction.

CHAPTER 11

Sexual Morality

The conference on Sexual Morality was only a week away, and Father John was fully prepared for the event. He confirmed this with Gloria at their next meeting.

"As you already, Father Michael is on board as the afternoon's keynote speaker. He tells me his speech will cover what the government is doing about reducing the incidence of teenage pregnancy, which includes rolling out some education programs and working to improve the economic conditions in poor communities.

Dr. Francesca plans to express her opinion on how to help control or reduce the incidence of early pregnancies, and she intends to emphasize the important role parents and school teachers can play in this regard.

"Our publicist has sent out invitations to many members of the local community, and distributed brochures in the poorer sections of the Bronx. There will be a TV camera recording the event to show on the religious channel, and three journalists plan to attend the conference.

"The police have been notified, and there will a number of officers stationed around the hotel and inside the hall. Everything else, including the food, stage work and the like, is in order.

Gloria beamed as she said, "Thank you, Father John! You have done a great job done already. Let us keep our fingers crossed, and pray that this conference helps bring about the desired outcome!'"

The next morning Gloria and Peter worked on her speech. Much of her intended talk highlighted the importance of the work yet to be done. Afterwards, Gloria spent the bulk of the day working reviewing myriad details of the conference with Father John. The two also discussed how she could best overcome any shyness as a first-time speaker in front of a large public group.

Late that same afternoon, Gloria visited Marco to discuss the Law of Attraction in depth. She started off by asking the question, "How do I reconcile my Christian faith—which I have no intentions of living without—and the teachings of Abraham on the Law of Attraction?'"

"From the little I know, Gloria, I believe they are inter-connected and not to be looked upon as two separate realms of spirituality. My understanding is you can be of *any* religious background and yet still be a believer in the Law of Attraction! So, you can go to church, or pray in a mosque or temple; no problem! The Law of Attraction clarifies and simplifies the understanding of your particular faith. It underscores the fact that you have the right to ask, believe and receive what you really want—which you learn how to achieve, or manifest, by virtue of your connection with your inner being. For example, if you are a Christian, you would be facilitating your relationship with the Holy Spirit when you pray and ask for what you really want.

"The Law of Attraction—or the Law of Vibration, which is what Abraham calls it—teaches us to be aligned with God, the Source of all Energy, and all that exists or is created. Of course, we have the choice to stay on the other side and think negatively—but if we do that, then that is what we would receive: negative results! It is all about our *choice*."

"Okay, I understand, but how do I combine these two schools of thought in.....one direction?"

"Little sister, don't look at them as two *diifferent* schools of thought when it comes to our daily way of life! For both schools of thought teach us that everything we think, every word we speak, and every action we take should represent our choice, which comes from either from a voice of love, or a voice of fear. Most of us should choose the voice of love—as Christ has said, and as all the other positive spiritual thought teachers say."

Gloria thought for a while, then said, "So, if I approach whatever I do in my daily life from the perspective or mindset of love, not fear, then I would be following the teachings of Christ as well as attracting like-minded people and things into my life?"

"Not only that, but you would also be inwardly connected with the Greater Mind, the Supreme Soul, the Universal Truth, and the Holy Spirit—all names meaning or signifying God. So, by following the teachings of Christ *and* by understanding and applying the Law of Attraction, you are coming full circle and living a life full of joy and peace!"

"Marco, are you sure you want to remain a businessman, and not become a spiritual philosopher and teacher? You amaze me with your depth of understanding and crystal-clear explanations! I am so proud of you, my brother, for what you just conveyed so clearly to me."

"Don't underestimate your own ability in this realm, my dear sister!" Marco said with a laugh. "For it is your life choices and deeds that inspired me to go on this path."

"Well, it is going to be a long and interesting path—perhaps even 'road less travelled'—but it sounds like it will be full of fun and rewards! I had better get going now, but please make sure you come to our conference next week!"

"We will all be there—Lula, the entire family and a host of other good friends," Marco reassured his sister.

"By the way, how is Lula? Any plans to go down a particular path together in the future?"

"So now you are getting curious about my relationship, like I am about yours! Lula is adorable, so intelligent and doing fine. I really love her, and I actually think we will get engaged soon."

"That's great news, Marco. If you do, I look forward to celebrating this wonderful event with you. 'Birds of a feather flock together!'"

The next day, Father John hurried into Gloria's office.

"Gloria, I wanted to tell you right away that the Mayor of New York City has agreed to come for the afternoon session to listen to Father Michael's speech! He told Father Michael, "I want to meet this young lady who is so benevolent!" So there you go! It's a done deal!"

"Great news, Father John. Perhaps we should notify the publicist to announce the Mayor's visit, as it may lead to greater media coverage of our event. My goodness, I do hope the ballroom will be big enough to accommodate more people!" Gloria worried.

"I already notified her, Gloria. And we also will have standing room in the back for another one hundred people if need be."

"Excellent to hear! Thanks again for your hard work, Father."'

Gloria was so elated to hear the news about the Mayor that she closed the door of her office to be alone for the next thirty minutes to pray and to revisit thoughts of her future mission.

The day before the conference Peter took Gloria out for dinner to soothe her nerves: She had become quite anxious about the day of the conference, and her own speech in particular. Peter encouraged her to be normal self, as she normally presents very well.

At 8:30 the following morning, Gloria and her family arrived at the hotel where the conference was going be held. A large number of people were already waiting in line for the doors outside the conference hall to open. Gloria introduced , whothe hotel an hour earlierwa, to her family.

Right before doors were opened to the public at 8:45 a.m., Diana and Emma ushered twenty-six girls sheltering in currently the Centers to some seats that had been reserved for them in the front of the main room. Then the doors were opened to the public, and the waiting crowd hustled inside to find seating.

The audience consisted of parents, teenagers, young children and several nuns, including Mother Superior and Sister Delores, as well as priests from different convents and churches in the area. Two policemen stood at the back of the room to ensure the safety of the event.

By nine a.m. the ballroom was full, with all three hundred seats taken. Father John was the M.C., and after walking up to the podium on the stage, he introduced Gloria Camino, the founder and head of the Mercy Centers.

Gloria was dressed in a light blue pantsuit over a white shirt, and she looked very elegant. After reaching the podium, she gave the following speech:

"Good morning Mother Superior, Sister Delores, Councilmen, ladies and gentlemen. My name is Gloria, and I welcome you to our one-day conference. I am pleased you could all join us to explore together an issue that we all want to see resolved.

The theme of our conference is "Sexual Morality." You may ask why we have chosen this topic or title

Well, what has gone on in our Christian Mercy Centers has been a great learning experience for me and my colleagues. Our first Center has been open for almost a year by now, and already we have treated about one hundred teenage girls. About 60 percent of those young ladies who came to us for help were pregnant—and some of them were as young as fourteen years old! Others came for assistance as they had either been abused by their parents or boyfriends, or been raped.

Teenage pregnancies, and abuse or violence directed against our young people, has become a huge epidemic in our society. Teenagers are generally ill prepared and still too immature to deal with the consequences of their actions. Socioeconomic conditions affect this situation, for the incidence of teenage pregnancy rises in those areas where the socioeconomic status is decreased or low. The root causes of that decreased status are low incomes and poor education.

On a national level, official surveys have shown that in the United States alone, there are close to one million pregnancies in women who are under the age of twenty. Over haf of them keep their babies, while about 40 percent choose abortions. Sadly, the United States has higher rates of teenage pregnancies than Canada and most European countries.

Our government's efforts to prevent unwanted pregnancies remain somewhat weak. The resulting health disparities caused by teen pregnancies afjfect both the child and the mother. I am sure we will hear more on the subject later from our honorable speakers, so I will pause now to simply ask the questions, 'How did this come about, and who or what is responsible for its continued growth? What can be done to stop it, and how do we go about doing so?'

The girls who came to be assisted by our humble Centers have told us their stories. From these first-hand accounts we have learned that there are three primary groups are responsible for not guiding these young girls in the right direction: Their parents, the schools and their houses of worship.

We also learned that there are two major reasons behind this lack of proper guidance: Poverty, and a lack of education.

While the government, on local, state and national levels, continues to develop the necessary programs in poor neighborhoods to uplift the standard of living in such communities, it is <u>not</u> enough. The real task necessary to improve socioeconomic conditions is for parents to set an example to their children by working hard to achieve decent living standards.

This responsibility of the parents should also be coupled with their encouragement to ensure the education of their children. They need to tell them not only to achieve good grades, but also to abstain from immoral sexual activity until they are married.

All good Christians know what the Bible teaches. If you don't, please do not hesitate to ask your church leaders to help you better understand these teachings about sexual activity.

In addition to the very important role that parents play, another very important role in our children's lives is that of the teachers in middle and high schools. It is my understanding that the schools mostly encourage kids of both genders to use contraceptives, or to guide pregnant students where to go f they want to have an abortion. I have to say this is not the right guidance or the proper advice! Our children's teachers should first teach them <u>to abstain from premarital sex altogether.</u> Teenagers should watch videos that show the horrors, results and risks related to sexual behavior at early ages, and how unhealthy it could be both for them and any babies that may result.

According to the National Campaign to Prevent Teenage Pregnancy, 87 percent of teenagers said it would be much easier for them to abstain from having premarital sex if they were able to have more open conversations with their parents and teachers.

Last but not least, I would like to emphasize the role all faith leaders can play in explaining and encouraging teens to understand the spiritual values and benefits of abstinence. For example, it would ideal for youth leaders in those churches that offer such groups to become involved in discussing sexual morality with their teenage members, and encourage them to reinforce their spiritual values. Both male and female teens need to learn about the importance of, and the church's expectation regarding, delaying sexual activity, pregnancy and parenthood until they reach the right age where they can become married first.

Some of you may wonder—and I am often asked—why I have chosen this work at such a young age. Why I don't have focus on having fun instead, and going out with my friends? I say in response, I am inspired by the Divine Power to proceed with this calling regardless of my age, I have fun, and experience the greatest joy, though helping others in need, I am a friend to all the girls who come to the Centers and to all those who work with me, I am blessed with a great family who believe in my mission and help provide me with the resources required to fulfill my dreams, I am determined to be a role model to all young people to change the way they think, the way they feel and the way they live, I am not afraid of what I do now or continue to do in my future, I work from a mindset of Love, not Fear, I have Faith in God that I will always be protected, and that 'with Him, all is possible,'

— *I believe that God sent me to live my life with a purpose, to serve Him and to bring the people that cross my path closer to His Love, and, I do not seek fame or fortune; I only seek God's Mercy and His continued Blessings for the work I do.*

I want to dedicate my life to empowering young people to become sef- dependent! I want them to learn how to have a life with a clear purpose, one that is based on sef-esteem. I desire them to have the faith that their dreams will be fulfilled, knowing always that God is on their side with His love and mercy.

Allow me now to ask the girls and my colleagues from our to stand so you can see them for yoursef and talk to them during the break if you wish.

Thank you!"'

The audience stood up again and applauded Gloria for a full minute. She bowed her head in thanks, and Father John took the microphone and asked if anyone has any questions. Many people raised their hands during the resulting Q&A session. Some typical questions were:

Q: *"How many Centers do you plan to have, and will they all be in the Bronx region?"*

A: *"We do not know how many exactly, but the plan is for at least another two in the Bronx. I hope this momentum continues so that more Centers open in the other four boroughs of New York City within the next couple of years. I also hope other people will do similar work in other states."*

Q: *"How are you financing your work?"*

A: *"We are a non-profit organization, and all our expenses are adequately funded by generous gifts and donations from people who are aware of our work. Special thanks to the volunteers who help us, including our certified registered nurses. They help keep our expenses low."*

Q: *"Do you get paid for your work?"*

A: *"No. I am a volunteer too."*

Q: *"How do you manage to survive without a salary?"*

A: *"I am grateful to my family for their love and support. They are present here with us today."*

Many curious mothers with their young daughters surrounded Gloria during the coffee and tea break that followed Gloria's speech. Many of the mothers applauded her for her 'important' and 'essential' work, and offered their help as Center volunteers in the future. After, Gloria's family and Peter came up to her and hugged her as they affirmed how proud they were of her.

Gloria began looking for Mother Superior and Sister Delores among the crowd. After a while, she found them talking with Diana and some of the girls from the Centers. Gloria waited patiently, and when Mother Superior noticed her, she turned to hug Gloria. She then told her what good work she was doing, and how important her words she spoke to the public had been.

Sister Delores reached out and did the same. The two then apologized they could not stay any longer, for they had to go back to the convent.

Gloria thanked them for coming and promised to visit soon.

Father John introduced the second speaker, Dr. Francesca, after the break. He emphasized her experience with pregnant teenage girls in particular, along with where she worked and her education, then encouraged the audience to listen carefully to her words of wisdom.

The doctor's speech was filled with examples of the young pregnant girls that she had treated, and specifically the miserable condition of their health and the health of their babies. She repeated the importance of education at home and in the schools, and that parents should open discussions with their children about the dangers of premarital sex. She also criticized church leaders for failing to have these essential conversations with members of their congregations. She then went on to share some statistics that proved that premature pregnancies were more prevalent in low-income neighborhoods.

In a decidedly upbeat voice, Dr. Francesca went on to say how valuable the work of the Centers has become within the Bronx! She referred to the Centers as "Oases of Love and Care" whereby the girls receive loving shortterm help and counseling before being sent to professional clinics and hospitals for long-term treatment and assistance. She asked the community to help out these centers by volunteering and donating money to ensure their continuity and growth.

The audience applauded Dr. Francesca's speech, and a twenty-minute Q&A followed. At the appropriate time Father John took the podium to inform the attendees that a complimentary lunch was available until two p.m.in one of the hotel's dining rooms.

At 1:55 p.m., the wail of sirens in the distance indicated the arrival of the Mayor of New York City and Father Michael, spiritual advisor to the Mayor. Father's Michael's speech would be the last of the day.

Gloria, Father John, Luca and the local chief of the police went to the hotel's to receive the two well-known figures. Gloria was thrilled to be introduced to the Mayor and Father Michael, both of whom congratulated her on her important work through the Centers.

The men walked with Gloria and Father John, who took them inside to the ballroom. Everyone inside the room stood up and began clapping the moment they saw the guests walk in towards the front section of the room.

Father John eagerly introduced his friend Father Michael When Father Michael took the stage, he greeted everyone, thanked the Mayor for joining the event, and said with a big smile, *"Let me first start with a joke that went like this:*

'There was a contest in a girl's high school. The students were asked to write a short story containing three words: religion, sex and mystery. So after few minutes, the girl who won the contest had written: "Oh God, I am pregnant! I wonder who did it."

When the crowd's laughter subsided, Father Michael said, *"While what I just said was a joke, isn't the situation that I described one that can and does happen to many teenage girls? They unexpectedly find out they are pregnant, and they have no idea who did it. Then they seek God's help to explain it all!*

Gloria, Father John told me about what you are doing and how you plan to expand your mission by opening more centers in crucial areas of our city. I, and on behaf of the Mayor who honored us with his presence today, commend you on your work and God will reward you man, fold.

Now, on the subject of sexual immorality, let me share with you what our government and what our churches are doing...."

For about twenty minutes Father Michael elaborated on the government and church programs intended to reduce the incidence of teenage sex and pregnancies. He supported his statements with statistics, and shared with the audience the new substantial budget and projects recently approved by New York City's Mayor to improve the socioeconomic status of poorer areas of the city. Among the projects were new public school education programs to educate high-school-age children on the importance of abstaining from sexual activity while young, and how sexual promiscuity without protection can be hazardous to their health and lives.

Father Michael's speech met with loud applause, and then there were twenty minutes set aside for questions. Many of the audience's questions came from parents who wanted to have more information about the specific education programs to which Father Michael had referred.

Before Father Michael stepped down, the Mayor climbed the stairs to the stage. Taking the microphone from Father Michael, the Mayor said a few words of gratitude for the work that had already been done on educating and assisting poor teens, then Gloria to join him on the stage. Gloria had no idea why he was asking her to join, but she went to the stage anyhow.

The Mayor greeted her and said, "Gloria, I am proud to give you a bronze medallion! It is the highest honor the City gives to its noteworthy individual civilian citizens. You have done a great job, and you have set a great example to all our young people, who hopefully will accomplish similar achievements in their lives.'"

The Mayor placed the medallion around her neck, then briefly hugged her. With tears pooling in her eyes, Gloria thanked him. The applause from the audience was quite loud, accompanied by whistles and cheers.

The conference then ended for the day, hopefully having accomplished its mission.

CHAPTER 12

A Different Way to Connect

After the conference, Gloria went home with her family and Peter. Luca had invited several people to a dinner at his home in her honor. The meal was being catered by his preferred Italian restaurant.

Luciano, the chief of police, Father John, and Gloria's cousin Eduardo were among the guests who congratulated her on her successful event. However, it was the first time Eduardo, who had a crush on Gloria, was meeting Peter. He knew that the two were close, and he could not help but be a bit jealous even though he knew he had no chance to have Gloria as his girlfriend, being that he was a member of her family. To distract himself this line of thinking, Eduardo started asking Peter about his studies at the Seminary, and what he intended to do once he got his doctorate degree in divinity.

Peter politely answered with, "To be completely straightforward, I don't have any specific plans yet. And I am not quite sure I will choose to serve as an ordained priest in a church.'"

"Why then are you taking courses in divinity?'"

"Well, Gloria and I have started discussing working together on some joint projects in the future, and I do not know if this kind of work that we have yet to figure out would require me to be ordained as a priest.'"

"Do you have any specific time frame as to when the two of you plan to work together? And would your plans include building some Mercy Centers together?'"

"Not necessarily, Eduardo. Actually, we are thinking of working on somewhat bigger projects that go beyond the current scope of the Mercy Centers. However, figuring out exactly what they are right now is a bit premature and daunting, as we are both still not finished with our studies. We hope to reach the decision once we graduate in about one year.'"

"So does this mean you do not have any interest in joining your father in his extensive real estate investments?'"

"No, not really. I have a different calling than my father, Eduardo, and I yearn to live a much more simple and meaningful life.'"

"I see," Eduardo said with a nod of his head. "I wish both of you the best with your plans, and it was really nice talking to you.'"

Peter breathed an internal sigh of relief when Eduardo stopped bombarding him with questions, and he went over to a corner of the living room to relax. Marco happened to be walking by, and he stopped to ask Peter if his cousin was a bit much with all the questions.

When Peter did not comment one way or the other, Marco told him, "Don't worry; Eduardo is a great guy, but he is of no threat to you. He has always loved Gloria, and always will. But as she is his first cousin, he has no hope of competing with you in the romance department.'"

Peter remained silent, but his eyes widened when he heard Marco's comment. had Eduardo admired in this way

It was later that evening when Peter got the attention of Gloria, as she had been talking to everybody else who had made demands on her time. The two friends sat down on a sofa in the large living room and Gloria asked him with a curious smile, "So, what do you think about the day and my speech Professor?'"

"Gloria, you stole the show!" Peter said warmly. "I noticed how you added some quite personal remarks and observations at the end, and that made your presentation truly magnificent. I am really proud of you and the way you spoke. You can relax now in the knowledge that you are one heck of a speaker! I was watching from the back, and I saw you fully engaged the attention of the audience when you spoke. They were listening attentively. And of course, you looked so beautiful and attractive on stage!'"

"Thank you, Peter!" Gloria said, color rising in her cheeks. "That also was nice of the Mayor to honor me with a medallion. I was really touched by his gesture.'"

"Gloria, it is not a gesture, but an honorable recognition of the great job you are doing. You truly deserve that award. Besides, wait until you see the subsequent media coverage on TV and in the papers; the news about what you are doing and accomplishing is bound to be picked up ! Don't let it get to your head, though," he cautioned, "as we have a lot more to do that lies ahead of us.'"

"Yes, of course," Gloria agreed. "Now, what was my cousin Eduardo talking to you about? I saw you having quite the discussion with him at the other corner of the room, but of course I couldn't heard what you were discussing from where I sat.'"

"He told me what a tough cookie you are, and then he almost cried because you broke his heart.'"

"What?" Gloria burst out, her eyes almost popping from their sockets.

"No, no, I am just kidding, Gloria," Peter grinned. "But clearly Eduardo thinks the world of you. He just wanted to know a bit more about me, to make sure that his cousin is seeing a decent man.'"

"I see," Gloria said, somewhat nonplussed. "Well, dinner is ready. Let us go eat, for I am hungry!'"

The conversation around the dining room table as everyone enjoyed their meal was about the conference and how productive it had seemed. The key question was whether the aftermath of such an event would bring about a change in the life and sexual behavior of teenagers. *Would parents, teachers and religious leaders work harder on explaining and discussing such subjects with teenagers?*

That was the challenge, and undoubtedly Gloria and those working at the Centers would find out in due course.

After dinner came to an end, Marco, Gloria and Peter stayed behind a bit longer to talk. Gloria asked her father if they could borrow the sitting area in his office, and Luca agreed.

It was the first time the three of them discussed together the spiritual message that Gloria was obsessed about figuring out for the future.

Once they settled down in some wooden chairs, Gloria started the conversation by saying, "As you may know, people are becoming less and less churchgoers on Sundays, which is a sign of their dissatisfaction with the routine rituals of the mass or service they attend. Meanwhile, I hear that more and more people are responding to the new teachings of Spirituality—just like you are, Marco —instead of the sermons the spiritual leaders offer from the more structured and traditional religions. My question is, *Is there is a conflict of interest here? Or to ask it differently, would I, as a Catholic Christian, be betraying my Christianity if I followed the new spiritual teachings?*"

Peter promptly responded with, "If I may add, one reason the attendance at churches is decreasing in this day and age of fast information is the fact that the Christian leadership is resisting any adaptations to the modern way of life. The leadership is not open- minded in terms of the increasingly popular new spirituality, especially when it is expressed or taught differently from what religious tradition teaches. The leadership continues to hold on rigidly to the old doctrines and rituals of the past.

"Yet people nowadays are seeking a different way of connecting with God; they desire to individually experience a connection with God, rather than follow the traditional way of finding that connection with fellow churchgoers during a mass or other service. It seems that the church that still believes there is more power in many together than in one alone.'"

Marco spoke up to say, "I like what you have noted, Peter, about the church finding power in the gathering of many rather than the power of one individual connection with God, or the Source of all Energy. To say it differently, and to go back to Gloria's question, there is no conflict at all if an individual who is connected with God evolves and radiates positive vibrations in a church atmosphere. To the contrary! This radiation of thoughts and good feelings is manifested in the person's positive outlook on life. This balanced vibrational alignment with the Source can only enhance the spirituality of other churchgoers, or even the church leadership.'"

Gloria said thoughtfully, "So you're saying that I—as a minister, let's say—would be capable of manifesting such energy and wellbeing from the pulpit when I preach, right? Not only by virtue of my behavior with people outside the church, but also inside it, for example, during a Mass service? Is that correct?'"

Marco gave a nod of agreement.

"Absolutely right, Gloria. A personal relationship by any church member or church leader with God can only enhance and foster belief within the community, for then the churchgoers are seeing that a 'connected' person is making real what the church has always been talking about! Yet many traditional religions normally hinder or obstruct such a personal connection to God, because most organized religions want to see what you, as a follower, can do for them, rather than seeing you independently empowered. They support the belief that 'individually we are weak, but in numbers we are more powerful.' Such religious teachings are frightening to many. But as 'connected' individuals, each one of us can manifest the opposite of fear by spreading unconditional love and radiating the power of the Universe.'"

Gloria said, "You see, Peter? I told you about Marco's new spiritual path, and now you are hearing it first-hand! That is why I wanted us to meet together: to see if we can come up with a directive to share with the average person that it is okay to remain members of our religious traditions, while simultaneously being tuned in and turned on, radiating our individual wellbeing.'"

Peter nodded.

"Through this discussion, I understand now more clearly that I can radiate my aligned spirituality without impacting my Christian beliefs. I would like to be an example to others, one who can teach people how to change the way they think and feel first.'"

"Well said, Peter! And may I point out that you are a fast learner!'" Marco observed with a genuine smile.

Gloria concluded the meeting by saying, "We should have more sessions like this with just the three of us. I hope the next one happens soon!'"

The next day, Father John monitored the TV channels and bought the local papers. He heard and read all the positive coverage that resulted from the conference event before he called Gloria and shared with her the good news. She asked him to read aloud to the headlines of three papers in particular:

* *The Bronx Chronicle,* and it read:
"*Our own Gloria Camino Honored by the Mayor of NYC*"
* *The New York Medical Journal,* and it read:
 "*Gloria Camino, Head of Mercy Centers, receives a Bronze Medallion from the City*"
* *The Bronx Daily,* and it read:
"*Gloria Camino, the new Princess of Our Teenagers* "

Father John promised to save the articles to show her, and make a copy of the TV coverage as well. Before he ended the call, Father John said she should expect to receive a host of emails and messages of congratulations from a multitude of new admirers.

After hearing this good news, Gloria wrote in her journal:

> *I will take this media recognition as a push to my momentum toward the expansion of the good deeds that I am guided to perform. I am grateful for the many blessings God has bestowed upon me. I feel more responsible now to add more bricks to the foundation of the new structure I envision building for the future.*
>
> *I will remain humble, grateful and astute while I continue on the path ahead. Again, my bigger dream is to come up with a unified message that encompasses the essence of good religious teachings with modern spiritual thoughts. I will remain focused, and it will come to me.*

Marco and Peter called a little later, and each happily conveyed to Gloria the same news that she just received from Father John. Both men said it is only the beginning of greater things that will evolve in time.

Gloria responded to both men by asking them to pray and give thanks to God, and to also ask Him to give her more strength to fulfill the task that lay ahead for her.

The next day when Gloria went to the office, Father John met her with copies of the media articles and a copy of the TV recording received from his friend at the station.

Gloria looked at him with a smile on her face and humbly said, "Thank you, Father John, for these, and the work you are doing to make the public aware of what they can do to keep down the incidence of teenage pregnancy. I am grateful, and also encouraged to pursue the mission God has set for me. Still, we have a lot of work ahead of us, and I am so happy you are at my side already.'"

"Gloria, I am honored to help you in your blessed endeavors, and I will be with you all the way. I have never enjoyed a better working relationship, and I find it very fulfilling. It is now close to nine o'clock, so be ready to receive a host of calls from reporters.'"

"Father John, please ask the reception board to forward all these calls to you. I am not good at such things, and I am certain you will do a better job than me.'"

"Okay, I will do what you say. I will sift through the list of callers and if something sounds interesting, I will bring it to your attention.'"

And indeed the phone rang all morning. Father John patiently took all of the reporters' calls, and answered many questions. There were fourteen callers that morning, most of whom asked if they could have an interview with Gloria at some time during the week. He said he would discuss the matter internally, and get back to them as soon as possible.

Father John called Gloria early that same afternoon.

"I have taken fourteen calls, most of which were from local, state and national newspapers. Two of the callers were from national TV networks, and one was from the *American Atheist Magazine.* I believe we had enough local coverage so I will decline the offer of interviews from those papers. But perhaps we can schedule interviews with the two national TV channels, two state papers, and two national papers? And of course, I suggest we decline the interview offer from *Atheist Magazine.* What do you think of this plan?'"

"All is fine with me, but I do want to meet with the reporter of the *American Atheist Magazine.* Please schedule it as well.'"

"But, Gloria. A' Father John objected, sounding bewildered at her response.

"No buts or ifs, Father John, and I can handle this one!" she said confidently. "I have no fear of anyone, remember?" Gloria teased.

"Okay, then," he capitulated. "I will spread out the interviews, with a maximum of two per day, and a maximum one hour each. Don't forget they undoubtedly will come with cameras and tape recorders!"

"Fine; that is no problem. You should feel free to show them the premises of both Centers as well. Thank you, Father John!"

Father John called back all reporters, and set up the interviews to which Gloria had agreed within a week's time. He then gave a copy of the schedule to Gloria.

The first interview was with PBS at 10 a.m. on Tuesday, and the second with the *New York Post* at three o'clock on Tuesday afternoon. The following days of the week were scheduled similarly, with the last interview being on Friday at three o'clock with the *American Atheist Magazine* reporter.

The interviews went well, with the reporters asking more or less the same questions in every interviews. Gloria answered the questions with confidence and humility, always ending with a message beseeching parents, schools and churches not to neglect their responsibilities towards today's teenagers.

The last interview was the somewhat controversial one Gloria had agreed to from the reporter of *Atheist Magazine*. Gloria sensed that the intention of the reporter was more to promote the magazine through riding on the back of her popularity, rather than a reflection of a genuine interest in her work…although to remain silent throughout

Some portions of the interview went like this:

Reporter: "Do you agree that the work you are doing is predominantly based on your compassionate and humanitarian feeling towards non-privileged teenagers?"

Gloria: "That is partly it; correct."

Reporter: "What do you mean, 'partly?' What are the other parts missing from your response?"

Gloria: "First and foremost, I owe my inspiration for my work to a divine guidance."

Reporter: "Do you mean you were inspired by a god?"

Gloria: "Absolutely, my God, and the only God; who else?"

Reporter: "Why? You don't think you can do this work without believing in a god?"

Gloria: "You would need to persuade me otherwise. I believe you can count on only one hand the projects full of love and mercy that were inspired and implemented by people who do not believe in God. I also do not know of any non-profit humanitarian organization founded and supported by people who do not believe in God! But you are the expert in the area of atheism, so do enlighten me if this is not the case. Hundreds of the humanitarian deeds and charities that exist today all originated from people who were inspired by a religious belief in God. If you think I am wrong without being able to supply evidence to the contrary, please feel free to contact such organizations and find out them yourself."

Gloria said these remarks with a facetious smile on her face, leaving the reporter dumbfounded, intimidated and embarrassed. The interview ended shortly thereafter, with Gloria doubting that the magazine would even print any excerpts or run any feature article. Gloria refused to allow this reporter to take advantage of her newfound fame and blemish it, and she did not desire to receive any sort of publicity that came from an atheist source.

Once the reporter left Gloria's office, with Father John showing him the exit, Father John came back to Gloria's office and said, "I was mesmerized by your articulate answers! They showed courage and belief in what you are doing. I bet this guy will not print an article on you and the work of the Centers."'

"I know, and I don't care," Gloria said candidly. "Do you think I need an opinion or article out there from an atheist magazine? It is likely he may alter the entire interview to his advantage and turn it around to serve the magazine's interest! Please keep an eye on what they report when the next issue is out next week. If the contents are different from what I said, I will sue the magazine for libel. You were here as my witness after all."'

Father John surprised Gloria then by pulling out a small recorder from his pocket and admitting that he had discretely recorded the interview. When he caught sight of Gloria's dumbfounded expression he said with a wry smile, "I've been around, you know!"'

"Father John!" Gloria laughed in bemusement and admiration.

On his way out Gloria overheard him say in a quiet voice, as if to himself, "I love this work!"'

Gloria had plans with Peter to have dinner with him and his parents at their place in the city, for, as Peter told her, they missed her and kept asking him about her all the time. So a few hours after the interview with the atheist reporter, Gloria went home first to freshen up and spend an hour or two with her own parents and Marco before the trip down to Manhattan.

When she sat down with them in the den, she found that they received copies of the local papers and the TV recording from Father John. They were all tickled with joy over the review coverage, and they expressed one more time how proud of Gloria and her humanitarian work they were.

As for Gloria, she did not take the coverage to heart or make a fuss about the positive remarks in the papers and the TV video, all of which referred to her as a 'hero of the Bronx!'

At one point Marco asked his sister about the last interview with the *Atheist Magazine*. After she relayed what had gone down, and her concerns, Luca spoke up.

"Sweetheart," Luca promised, "if the magazine chooses to ever falsify your statements, I will make sure they pay dearly for it!:"

"Father, cool down!" Gloria placated. "I actually have something unexpected to tell you...something that was quite the surprise to me! I asked Father John to be present at the interview as a witness, and afterwards, he told me had discretely recorded the entire session, for he had similar fears!"

"Gloria, I quite like that Father John, and in more ways than one!" Luca replied with a broad grin. "Anyhow, if something does happen, I am prepared to have my lawyers to handle the case for you if it were to go that far!"

"Thank you, Father, for your unwavering support. For now, let me go freshen up as it's almost time to head into the city to dine with Peter's family."

Gloria went upstairs to get ready while Luca had asked his driver to be on standby to escort her.

CHAPTER 13

Generous Gifts

The second visit with Peter's family proved even more enjoyable than the first one. Joseph and Monica were very welcoming, and at ease with Gloria and Peter together. The love between them was radiant and conspicuous.

They group shared a meaningful conversation around the dinner table during which the Shepards explained they had read all the articles Peter had shown them about Gloria and her work. Joseph told her he was most impressed by the one which appeared in *The New York Post*. In it the reporter had complimented Gloria, citing her "depth of understanding as to what human benevolence is all about, despite her very young *age.*"

Joseph then looked to Gloria and asked, "How do you feel about your accomplishments so far?"'

"I am grateful for what has been done and accomplished, but I also look forward to the continuation of my spiritual journey in the future."'

"How do you receive your guidance, if I may ask?" Joseph inquired.

"Well, when I wake up every morning, I first prepare myself to accept a new day full of miracles. The key to guidance is awareness or consciousness of our higher self, for it is with us every moment. I train myself to be connected with my higher self as often as I can. I find this process to be a good source of guidance for the actions and decisions that await me during the day."'

"Does one have to be spiritual to achieve that?" Joseph wondered.

"The practice of having this awareness is an act of spirituality by itself,"' Gloria explained. "Spirituality, from my experience, is not something we learn, but a belief of accepting that we are part of a greater universal power, and all we have to do is to try and connect with that Source. It is not a religion or label, but the process of our individual desire to be aware of the way we think, feel, and act. If we are engaged in such, miracles flow naturally and appear in our everyday life!

"A miracle is when we see a smile on the face of those who are ill, when we feed someone who is hungry or thirsty, and when we have a conversation that we can learn from, and so on. It is not something 'magical' that happens.'"

Peter, who was listening quietly to the conversation between Gloria and his father, felt his insides inflate with renewed admiration for Gloria's clear and insightful thoughts and articulate delivery.

At this point Monica stepped in and said in a somewhat coy tone, "I don't mean to interrupt this wonderful conversation, but I am eager to ask how you two are getting along! It has been about six months now since the two of you have known each other; is all going well the way you wished?'"

"Peter, why don't you respond to your mother's question please?" Gloria said, her cheeks becoming quite pink.

"Clearly," Peter said, shaking his head, "my mother, whom I dearly love, is an eager beaver who is counting on us to be together in a more. socially acceptable, shall I say, capacity! Am I right Mom?'"

Without waiting for a verbal response from his mother, Peter continued, "Well, my friend Gloria can speak for herself, but as far as I am concerned, I am the happiest man on earth to be a close friend of this amazing young woman. I am so blessed and grateful that she has accepted me in her life. Let me say that we are very good work and social partners, and also that our relationship is flourishing from within. We trust God for its continuity and continued growth. Does that satisfy your curiosity, Mother?'"

"Peter, I am glad to hear what you have said! It's just that your father and I can't wait to see the two of you become a couple," Monica admitted. "We believe that the two of you being together is a miracle by itself!'"

Gloria then spoke up.

"Monica, I truly appreciate what you have just said. Candidly, Peter and I are aware of a potential future together, and we discuss it from time to time. We enjoy each other's company and we have a lot of fun when we are together. We are so relaxed with each other, yet also confident through knowing that a greater power than ours means for us to be together! We do intend to spend the rest of our lives together, but we are taking care not to rush ahead of ourselves and our education here. We both will finish our higher education in about six months, and once this is behind us, we plan to address the situation more. attentively.'"

"Thank you so much for explaining! We have been thinking about it since we first met you and saw you together, and we wish you both the best of luck and happiness," Monica said.

Joseph then said, "I want you both to know how dear you are to us. We will patiently wait for you two to decide the next step.

"On a completely different subject—and I am also speaking on behalf of my wife Monica—I wanted to tell you, Gloria, that in support of your wish to expand your Mercy projects, or any other project you have planned, I am donating a 14,000 square foot space in Queens to your organization; it will become vacant in six months. You may do with it whatever you see fit. Its location is no more than a twenty-minute ride from your work in the Bronx or Manhattan.'"

Tears welled up in Gloria's eyes, and she got out of her chair to hug Joseph and Monica.

"Thank you! Thank you so much for this very generous gift." Gloria looked over at Peter with the tears still in her eyes before she looked back at his parents and said, "Peter and I will figure out together how best to use this amazing gift in due course.'"

"It may be helpful to know that the space is a single building that consists of three floors and a full basement," Joseph advised Gloria. "It has a small garden, and a decent parking area sufficient for seven cars. So it could be used as a clinic, an orphanage, a school, or anything else you like. When you have a chance, the two of you may want to go see it. I am not even sure Peter knows where it is. When you decide what to do with the space, just let me know, and I will have it redone and furbished the way you like.'"

Peter could not hold back any longer.

"Mom and Dad, I don't know what to say. This is an act of true spiritual benevolence on your part, and I am sorry, for I misjudged you before! I did not think that you would do such a generous thing for us or anybody else. Gloria and I will definitely plan a great project. It will honor your name, and prosper with your blessing.'"

The four enjoyed dessert and coffee in the living room before Gloria signaled to Peter that it was time for her to go back home. She exchanged long hugs with both parents, and told Peter she will be seeing him in her office tomorrow. Then she went outside to the car and driver waiting to bring her home.

Peter stayed with his parents for another thirty minutes. They expressed how much they loved Gloria already, and how she had inspired and influenced them to have a more positive outlook on life. Joseph then told his son not to worry about a home for him and Gloria when they decide to live together one day; they can choose any apartment in any of the buildings he owns. Peter expressed his gratitude before excusing himself to return to his own place.

Gloria spent the next day going through a host of emails and text messages from more fans and volunteers. Donations were pouring in, and both Centers were fully occupied. Father John had to turn down further referrals from the police department, for it would be at least four more days until there were vacancies. Gloria realized that they had outgrown the current spaces, and needed to open up two more Centers in the Bronx within short order. She discussed her plan with Peter when he arrived early in the afternoon. They agreed they should talk it through further with Luca and Marco, who could help them to find them new space.

Gloria called Marco, explained what was on her mind and asked him if he could meet with them after work. He indicated his availability, and suggested they meet at the Camino mansion so they could involve their father in the discussion. They agreed to meet around six p.m., and when they told Gloria's mom, Luisa requested they stay for dinner.

Before they sat down at the dining table, Gloria explained to her father that the Mercy operation had outgrown its two spaces and she would like to find two more spaces and open new Centers simultaneously.

Marco had come prepared with a list of the spaces he and his father owned—all of which were currently occupied—as well as another list of the spaces they had that were available to rent or buy. Those that made this list were spaces not too close to the existing Centers, but spread apart to some degree.

Luca took a moment to look at the list of the ones available to buy; he noted there were two with about 6,000 square feet each. Marco had written down that one was in a bad shape, and the other in an acceptable condition. Both were townhouses in two different locations located about ten minutes apart form one another.

"Son, how much do each of these buildings cost?" Luca inquired.

"The total asking price for these two buildings is close to one million dollars" Marco answered.

"Marco, visit them with your architect friend and come back to me with a plan of how long it will take to renovate and refurbish them. If the sellers are unwilling to wait until you finish checking the spaces out, just go ahead and buy them both outright."

"Sure, Dad, I will go work on this right away. I will revert within a day or two once I check the spaces out with the architect. Gloria and Peter, if you wish, you are welcome to accompany us," invited Marco.

Peter and Gloria were speechless for the moment, so astonished were they by the willingness and ability of both their fathers to make such generous decisions so very quickly. Finally, Gloria moved over to sit on her father's lap, and she gave him a hug as if she were still a young child.

"Dad, I don't know why I am so lucky to have you as my father! I thank you for your great generosity, and I know God will reward you abundantly for it. Peter's father, whom you should meet soon, told us yesterday that he is donating to our organization a 14,000 square foot building in Queens that will be vacant in six months. God has blessed both Peter and me with such amazing parents!"

Then they all proceeded to have dinner together. Luisa made the best Italian pasta ever, and they all ate wholeheartedly.

After an enjoyable meal full of laughter and pleasantries, Gloria, Peter and Marco agreed to move to the living room for some more discussion on the subject of combining new spirituality and traditional religion.

Marco started with, "Gloria, it has been quite an eventful week, starting with the conference, then the interviews and finally the decision to open more Mercy Centers. How do you feel about all this?"

Gloria answered, "What else can I say other than we are so grateful at the Centers that we could accomplish so much in such a short period of time!"

Peter offered, "I am particularly blessed that I chose the path of spirituality for my life, as that choice is responsible for introducing me to the both of you! I now consider you both to be very close friends, and also my collaborators in an amazing future that I envision to be very productive and enlightening.'"

"It is thanks to Gloria and her courage that we are all pursuing a different road for our journey in life," Marco said. "Now to get back to our earlier discussion, let me inform you as to how fast the development and evolution of the new spiritual teachings has been. The publisher Hay House, founded by the late Louisa Hay close to forty years ago, holds what they call the 'Hay House World Summit' in the month of May.

This summit extends the teachings of more than one hundred spiritual world leaders and teachers in a series of speeches and books, many of which are accessible online to anyone interested in expanding their spiritual pursuits.

"All in all, the growth of new spirituality that has mushroomed over the last thirty years is unprecedented and exponential, and should be sending a strong signal to all organized religions to become more open-minded and accept that these newer practices will only enhance their own religious practices.'"

"That is good to know, Marco," Gloria replied. "I know that we may not be able to read or listen to the material of all these new spiritual leaders right away, so it could be helpful if you were able to recommend a few of them for Peter and me to familiarize ourselves with."

"It is interesting you ask such a thing, little sister, as I am working on such a selection for myself too! Many of the spiritual teachers are already well- known as they have written self-help books and given seminars and webinars on spirituality. Dr. Wayne Dyer, who recently passed away, is an example. He started out writing self-help books, and he has sold more than fifty million copies of his sixty-plus books. Then he turned into a highly respected spiritual writer in the last fifteen years of his life.

"Dr. Deepak Chopra is another example of a physician-turned-spiritualguru. He has written more than sixty-five books already, and remains very active in this field. I could mention a few others as well, all of whom essentially preach the same sermon, which is based on the individual's endeavor to connect directly with God, or the Creator, or the Source."

Peter asked, "How many different names do these new spiritual leaders have for 'God'?"

"Many! In addition to the ones just mentioned, there are, 'True Self,' 'Higher Self,' 'Holy Spirit,' 'Source Energy,' 'Creator,' 'Allah,' 'Universal Truth' and 'Supreme Soul.'" You may be interested to know that all of the leaders of the new spirituality admit that they are the same as what we call 'God.'"

"Why don't they all agree to call Him 'God' only?'"

"It's a good question, and I don't know the actual answer. But perhaps it is to differentiate the name from that used in the older established religions where God is revered as a distant Being?'"

Gloria said thoughtfully, "So, Marco, do you agree that Peter and I need to spend more time studying these new teachings to absorb their essence before we can create a message that would 'fit all sizes?' As you know, by that I mean to establish one simple language that can be understood and accepted by people from all different walks of life."

"Yes, I agree with that process, more or less," Marco answered.

"I wish there was a simpler way!" Gloria confessed with a half-laugh. "I hope I personally can find the time to pursue this additional study on top of my current courses! Is it at all possible for you two to do this extra work on my behalf, as I truly need to focus on the expansion of my current Center work?'"

Marco concluded the session, saying: "Yes, absolutely! No worries, Gloria dear; you focus on your mission, and we will do this homework, right, Peter?"

Marco arranged with a real estate agent to see the two available townhouses that Sunday. Gloria was able to go see them, and she chose to bring along Father John as well. Marco brought along his friend the architect.

They very much liked the first one they saw, as it did not require a lot of work and could easily accommodate seven bedrooms for fourteen girls to sleep in on its upper two levels. The bathrooms did need updating, but the lower two levels looked adequate to house two offices, a kitchen and a dining room.

As for the second space, it needed to be gutted in order to become a workable space for the Centers. So Marco managed to negotiate quite a good deal on the asking price for the second one. It ended up being that the total cost for both buildings, before any repairs and renovations, was under $800,000, and the architect said the remaining $200,000 in their budget would be more than sufficient to turn the two spaces into working Mercy Centers.

The new Centers were ready soon; the first, in thirty days, and the second, in sixty days. would be, and the relevant affiliates and the police were notified that they could start sending more girls for assistance.

Father John and Gloria started looking for volunteers, as well as a manager for each Center. Father John sifted through the emails from those who offered to volunteer, and soon thereafter made his selections.

Father John temporarily took over the responsibility of handling the affairs of the Centers so that Gloria could focus on her final exams, which were being held in one week's time. She did not visit or talk much with Peter during this time, as he also was extremely busy writing his Doctorate thesis, which needed to be submitted in two weeks. He chose as the topic of his thesis, Christianity vs. New Spirituality.

Marco assisted him with the subject of Spirituality, while Peter researched the Bible for the references to spirituality, most of which came from the New Testament.

A few weeks' later, Gloria graduated with a Master's degree in Religious Studies with honors.

As for the acceptance of his thesis, Peter had to undergo a verbal interview with three professors, all of whom had Doctorate of Divinity (DD) degrees. Two of the interviewers were leaders of established churches, and the questions they asked Peter were particularly grueling. Clearly they had formed their questions with the intent of refuting Peter's arguments that New Spirituality enhances the practice of the Catholic faith, rather than detracting or distracting from it.

After two long hours of undergoing questioning, Peter would have to wait a few days before he heard the final result.

When Peter called Gloria to fill her in, he told her that the had been quite narrow-minded, and adamant in terms of clinging to old rigid religious beliefs.

"Gloria, they resisted my idea that the practice of Christian doctrines in today's times now requires complementary spiritual support from other teachings. I think they might fail me," he worried.

Gloria replied, "First, you should put the thought of success in your mind. If you *think* you will fail, then you *will* fail! Remember: *Ask and you shall receive!* Now, Peter, just suppose they don't honor you with a doctorate degree...Is this going to keep you from moving forward without it?"'

"Sweetheart, I studied five long years to get this degree, and I deserve it. But if I don't get it, it will not change my opinion about following through on our future task together, no! I abide by what my True Self guides me to do, and that is more importnat than any degree."'

"Okay, i's so good you know that, Peter! So let us not worry about it then. We will know in a couple of days anyhow," she counseled.

On the third day after his interview, Peter was called in to meet with the same panel for the final decision on his thesis. The three professors were seated together behind a long table, with Peter asked to sit in a chair about twelve feet away in the center of the big room.

The head of the panel said, "We have discussed your paper during the past couple of days, and the majority of us has agreed to accept the contents of your thesis without any required changes. Mr. Shepard, we have never had to review such a challenging work from any of our other students! In regards to your thesis, we respect how you upheld our Christian faith, while also noting that the positive benefits of New Spiritual thoughts can be used to enhance your faith's credibility. We commend you on a job well done. Congratulations are in order!"'

At this, all three professors stood up. Peter got up and moved forward to thank them and shake their hands.

When Peter left the room, he spied Gloria anxiously awaiting him in the hallway. As soon as she saw the smile on his face and his right thumb pointed upward, she knew that he had passed. She ran up to offer a big hug.

"Wow, what a relief! I feel so much...lighter now, my dear Gloria!" Peter enthused.

"Congratulations! The acceptance of your thesis is a sign that we both are on the right track in terms of pursuing a new future full of fresh new spiritual ideas."'

"I am also so excited that now that we are both finished with our academic disciplines, we can freely think about a new path for our future together. Let's go out to a nice restaurant and celebrate this new life of ours. I can pick you up from home around seven p.m.; is that okay with you? We then can go to your favorite Italian restaurant."'

"The timing you propose is great, but let us to go to a more fancy restaurant I know," Gloria said with a warm smile. "We both deserve it after such a long wait."

At seven p.m. sharp, Peter stood at the door of the Camino mansion dressed in a dark blue suit. He looked very handsome indeed, so much so that when Marco opened the door for him, he shouted, "Wow! Gloria, you have got to come see this!"

Marco had not seen Peter so formally dressed before.

Despite Marco's call, it took Gloria another five minutes to make it down the stairs. As she descended the staircase, she saw the two young men chatting and Marco offering warm congratulations to Peter in the foyer.

Gloria dazzled in her new red silk dress. Her hair was swept up, and her face beautifully made up. Her mother walked down behind her, just as Luca emerged from his study. Both offered Peter their good cheers, and called him, 'Dr. Shepherd' to show their respect for Peter having received his Doctor of Divinity degree.

The young couple went to a French restaurant Gloria had the pleasure of enjoying from time to time. The food was delicious; the presentation, exquisite.

When dessert was served, they decided to celebrate with a glass of champagne as well. After Gloria took a sip or two from her glass, Peter unexpectedly got off his chair and went down on his left knee in front of Gloria. He pulled out a small light blue velvet box, opened it and pulled out a gorgeous diamond ring.

"Gloria, I have loved you since the moment I first saw you! Our friendship that ensued is an answer to my prayer. I love you today more than I loved you yesterday, and I will you love tomorrow more than I love you today. As God is my witness, and with all these people watching us, I ask you, my sweet Gloria, 'Will you marry me?'"

Her lips trembling with joy and surprise, Gloria immediately gave her answer. "Yes, I will!'"

Peter put the ring on her right hand, then stood up so the two could kiss each other on the lips for the first time. The other guests in the restaurant clapped their hands as the two sat down to toast their new engagement with more of the champagne.

"Peter, when did you have time to find this gorgeous ring?'"

"I told my mother about my intention to propose to you this evening, and she took me right away to Tiffany's, to meet with the jewelry manager there. I asked him to show us the best diamond ring he had—and you have it here! I have no idea how much my mother ended up paying for it, but she did so with great joy. She is so happy for us! So enjoy it, and we will go see them later in the week. She will love to see it on your hand, as do I!'"

"Oh, Peter, I am so thrilled and so grateful to you and your great parents. I can't wait to tell my own family! Let us leave very soon so we can catch them before they retire.'"

Marco, Lula, and Gloria's sister Maria were enjoying a late meal at the Camino mansion with Luca and Luisa when Gloria walked in and stood quietly on her mother's side of the table. She flashed her ring when Peter came up close behind her.

Those eating shouted joyously, "Mamma Mia!" and stood up to congratulate the newly engaged couple. Luisa, Lula and Maria kept looking at and complimenting Gloria on her sparkling diamond ring.

Peter felt somewhat shy, and he hardly said a word. He just stood there and held Gloria's non-jeweled hand with a huge smile on his face.

After about an hour, Peter excused himself to drive back to Manhattan. Once he left, Luisa asked her daughter if she and Peter had decided on a wedding day.

"Not yet, but it could be sooner than expected. It will be much harder for us to continue to live apart, and also abstain from physical togetherness, now that we are engaged."

Luisa then inquired, "Do you know where you and Peter might live when you get married?'"

"Most probably in Manhattan, partly because Peter's father offered us an apartment of our choice in any of the many prime buildings he owns, and partly because that might well be an easier location for managing our work in the future. And by the way, I think we should arrange for you and Dad to meet Peter's parents now that we are engaged.'"

Luisa nodded her agreement as Luca changed the direction of the conversation. He asked Gloria if she was continuing to receive calls or messages about her work, and whether she had heard anything about the *Atheist Magazine.*

"According to Father John, we will know Monday if they are going to print an article on me or not," Gloria replied. "As regards the other callers, the answer is yes. We have a list of several reporters to whom we have not yet had a chance to respond. I have also received several requests to be a keynote speaker in certain conferences. I will try and find time next week to attend to all of these matters."

Gloria met with her fiance the next day and the two agreed that the two families should meet very soon. In fact, Peter said he had already brought up the same thing with his parents the night before, and they had responded that they would like the Caminos to come visit them in their Manhattan home this coming Saturday. Gloria said that she would confirm it with her parents, but she felt that the date would be work.

Peter then asked her to go with him to visit the building his parents had donated in Queens. He said the current tenants had been informed of the plans for the building, and someone in the company's HR department was willing to give them a tour of the facility.

They agreed to drive over right away.

Gloria sat next to Peter in his car, and he drove over the bridge towards La Guardia Airport. He turned right before the airport exit to begin looking for the building, and when he found the address, they parked across the street since the building's parking lot was full. Then they crossed over towards the main entrance, which was comprised of glass doors from floor to ceiling.

The building was impressive on the outside, despite being built nearly thirty years ago. When Peter and Gloria entered, they gave the name of the HR person to the guard at the information desk in the lobby. Five minutes later, a middle-aged man walked towards them.

Alan Rokie introduced himself as the head of Human Resources for the company that occupied the space. He showed them around, starting with the basement. His company was using half that level presently as a storage space for files, with the rest of the space offering a cafeteria and a kitchen.

Then they went up the stairs and checked out the open spaces floor by floor. Alan told Peter and Gloria that forty people worked in the building, with most of the employees using cubicles. There were an additional five rooms used by top management and for conference rooms.

Peter and Gloria thanked Alan for showing them around at the end of the tour, then headed out.

As Peter started driving Gloria back to the Bronx , she said, "You know what, Peter? I do not believe this space should be used as a Mercy Center for teenage girls. The thought that comes to my mind is to turn the space into an Education Center. I would like to call it 'Shepherd Awareness Center,' or SAC for short. How does this idea sound to you?"

"What a great idea, sweetheart! It is time to move forward and educate people to have and acquire new thoughts and life qualities based on spiritual teachings. So yes, let's become educators! I really, really like that. We can ask the architects to plan out classrooms, as well as some offices for the instructors, and for you and me."

"I am so happy to see you so 'tuned in' already, Peter! These are my thoughts exactly. So this is your first big project of our mutual projects to work on. I think you should run the Center, my dear, and I will be your shadow. By the way, when can we talk about our big day?"

"Now you're talking," Peter said, his eyes sparkling with eagerness. "I am ready any day you choose! Even tomorrow is fine with me."

"Wow, you seem really excited to get it over with!" Gloria teased her fiance. "Take it easy, tiger; brides need time to prepare! This will be a big wedding, and I need a month or two at the very least!"

"I can help. Just tell me what you need, and I'll do it."

Gloria looked at him and burst into laughter.

"Okay, I would like you to choose my wedding dress, the outfits for the bridesmaids and the flower girls, the church and the venue, and the dozen or so other things that go along with that!"

Peter rolled his eyes before he said, "Gee, I had no idea that our wedding would be so complicated!"

"Peter, I know that you and I would not mind a small event, but do you really think our dear parents would agree? You are their only beloved son, and I am the last unwed child of my parents! Big days such as weddings are primarily for the family members to enjoy. So how about this? Let's have you and I focus on the date, then hire aright wedding planner to do the rest!"

"You are right, my dear Gloria. But I must admit, I still don't want it to be too big or flashy!"

"No problem, then. I will ensure it will be a quality event, not an ostentatious or extravagant one.'"

And the newly engaged couple smiled at each other, minds and hearts united in perfect agreement.

CHAPTER 14

A More Complete Vision

There was a five-foot color banner hanging with the word 'Congratulations!' in the front hallway of the second Center.

Marco had informed Diana in the morning of her engagement the night before, so Diana had made the handwritten banner together with Father John. The two then notified the girls in the second Center, and bused over the girls form the first Center. Everyone was standing together, and all started clapping when the newly engaged couple walked in.

Diana then told everyone to proceed to the dining area, where a large cake celebrating the engagement was ready for all to share.

This cheerful and positive event meant a lot to the girls. It allowed them to see first-hand the value in doing things properly. They enjoyed cake and laughter for about forty minutes, during which Father John asked "Dr. Peter" to give a small speech.

Peter used the occasion to tell everybody how much he loved his new 'boss,' Gloria. Hearing this, the girls all giggled! Then he said that although he and Gloria were officially engaged, they both had agreed to continue to abstain from any physical union until they get married.

"Young ladies, my relationship with Gloria has been the biggest gift God has given me! For our more than six months together, Gloria and I both knew that we were attracted to one another. We could have enjoyed a physical union together; no one could have stopped us if that was our choice. But also we both know and appreciate the value of patience, and Gloria and I are the kind of Christians who act on what we believe.

"Abstinence, or refraining from sexual intercourse, does require some self-control. It is human to be tempted, yet Gloria and I have abstained from going down that road. We are now engaged, and we will get married sometime soon. We have no desire to rush into going to bed together. We are blessed with so much compassionate work to do, and that keeps us focused and in control.

"Young ladies, each night before you go to sleep, start imagining a wonderful future for yourselves, wherein you *live a life with a purpose*. Try to focus on how you can help others, and how to live a moral and decent life. To do this, consider pursuing some more education or learning a new skill so that more job opportunities open up for you. Change the way you used to think—and your life will change as a result of your new thoughts as well!

"Let our story serve as a valuable example to you and your friends. Believe me, it is worth waiting for the right time and the right person!'"

The girls clapped and thanked Peter with a standing ovation.

After the party, Father John asked to speak with Gloria and Peter in her office. Once they were seated, Father John mentioned that Gloria had been invited to be a keynote speaker at three different national conferences—in New York City, Chicago and Pittsburgh—over the next two months. The conferences had a theme in common: morality and teenager behavior.

"Any resulting publicity would further cement your voice as a spiritual activist in the field," Father John advised.

"I understand that, but I would like to manifest a different and larger role than just someone who cares to help teenage girls abstain from premarital sex and pregnancies. I would like to convey an image that is bigger than just that. I've come to realize my calling is to empower youth of all ages, gender or socioeconomic status. I want them to focus on the root of the problem, not its outcome.'"

"That's perfect, Gloria, and the new stages with which you will be provided will be ideal platforms for you to express this. Use the podiums to explain how your purpose in life has helped you to evolve, and that your wish is to move beyond a limited and specific problem area that young people face —teenage pregnancies— to present a higher, more complete vision with a focus on the roots of the problems that young people face. Reiterate what are common, noble and honest values and morals, and encourage all to observe, teach and follow these values, which should be taught at home, in schools or in churches. You preached those values in our conference here, actually," he observed.

"Father, well said! You have become an expert on the subject yourself Perhaps I should recommend you to go in my place?" she said mischievously.

"My dear Gloria, it is you they want," Father John said warmly, without a hint of envy. "People want to see the halo that is around you when you speak. They hear a divine voice talking to them through you. Please help me here, Peter; am I right or not?'"

"Father John is right, sweetheart! You have a mesmerizing presence when you are on stage, and your ability to attract such full and complete attention from your audience when you speak is a unique gift. Besides, the increased publicity you would derive from being on a national stage would be timely, given what we just discussed after our visit to Queens.'"

"Okay, you two, I am convinced!" Gloria laughed happily. "And I promise I will handle it with a humble heart and an alert mind. Go ahead and book them all, Father! I cannot go in the opposite direction of my calling.'"

Father John was thrilled to hear this, and he left to accept the invites and arrange her travel schedule. A second later, he spun around on his heel and walked back in.

"I forgot to tell you, Gloria and Peter, the third Center will be ready next week. I notified our collaborating affiliates and the local police. I also hired a retired nurse I know to manage the place and sleep on the premises. The architect has already planned for a special bedroom for her next to the other six bedrooms that are able to accommodate up to twelve girls. Mrs. Bolton has agreed to a modest salary. I also selected two other daytime volunteers to assist her in running the operation. When you have time, let me know, so I may introduce them to you.'"

"I actually am free tomorrow morning," Gloria said, "and thank you, Father John. Again I must say, I don't know how I could manage without you. You are God's gift to me!'"

"I am flattered, and I congratulate you both again, on your engagement and your mutual graduations.'"

Once he left, Gloria and Peter nestled together on the sofa in her office and started checking dates on the calendar. It was already May, and they decided the third Saturday in June would be ideal. Gloria would be twenty-two by then, and Peter twenty-six. They decided they would leave it up to their parents to choose the venue after the parents met for the first time this weekend.

Peter then stayed with Gloria until she was ready to go home. He drove her there, happy that, at last, he was free to spend considerable more time with her.

At the Camino home, everyone in Gloria's immediate family was gathered, along with Lula and Maria's husband. Luisa insisted that Peter stay to have dinner with them: "You are a member of the family now."'

Peter told the group about his parents' invitation, and extended it to all who were present.

"It will be a nice celebration," Peter said, "and an occasion to meet the other side of the family."'

Marco, Peter and Gloria had a short conversation together after dinner. Marco briefed them that he had read some books recently that he highly recommended, namely:

- *I Can See More Clearly* by Dr. Wayne Dyer, in which Dyer finally explains his life transformation from a teacher of self-help to a highly influential spiritual wisdom leader.
- *The Power of Your Subconscious Mind* by Dr. Joseph Murphy, in which Murphy combines his spiritual wisdom as a priest with scientific research and findings to explain the influence of the subconscious mind on every aspect of people's daily life.
- *Becoming Supernatural* by Dr. Joe Dispenza, in which the scientist and a modern-day mystic leads his followers into becoming supernatural in their everyday life by practicing powerful guided meditations.
- *Reinventing the Body, Resurrecting the Soul* by Dr. Deepak Chopra, in which the famed doctor emphasizes how the soul actually creates the body, as people's cells are invisible ingredients of awareness and energy.
- *A Course in Miracles Made Easy* by Alan Cohen, who literally makes the 1976 classic, *A Course in Miracles*— about the self-study needed for spiritual transformation to find the way to Universal Love—easy to understand.

Cohen refers to God as 'Spirit,' shows his readers how to master the journey from fear to love, and reveals how the 'Course' speaks for all religions, not only Christianity.

Marco then told Gloria, "These books, along with the one I told you about before, *Ask and It is Given* by Esther and Jerry Hicks, are written by internationally recognized spiritual teachers, and represent a small but considerable part of hundreds of books out there and available by other great teachers. All are expressed in different styles, yet all consider their teachings of spiritual awareness to only complement—not contradict!—traditional religious beliefs.'"

"Peter, thank you so much for this list! I can't wait to read them, and hopefully learn from them," Gloria enthused.

"Yes, I am excited to read them over the ensuing months now that I have so much more time," Peter affirmed.

They then confided in Marco about their decision to use the Queens building gifted by Peter's parents as a place of education Center, instead of a clinic or a treatment Center.

Marco was excited to hear the news. "I can already envision filling up the shelves of this new Center with hundreds of spiritual books just like the ones I've recommended!'"

"I like your idea of a huge library, Marco, one full of spiritual teachings and self-help books. Peter, let's turn the building's first level into a library open to people who walk in; they can either read on the premises, or and take the books out to study at home. The other two floors can be offices, a big lecture room, and other classrooms.'"

Both men loved the new idea, and agreed to plan for it accordingly. Peter then said, "I will inform my father of our decision later, and I feel confident we can go ahead and furbish the building the way we envision it starting now.'"

The three of them had become one strong unit with a unified voice.

After wishing Marco and Peter a good night, Gloria went upstairs to her room and excitedly wrote down in her journal:

> *I am so grateful to God for the changes that are taking place in the lives of people whom I love. I am grateful for knowing clearly the purpose of my life, and what will be my life's journey.*

In this house, my father has been transformed into a forgiving and giving person who has regained his faith in God, which now accompanies the firm and abiding faith of my mother Luisa. It is amazing how Marco has changed his life, converting from a more secular life to a joyous spiritual path on which he travels with his girfriend Lula. And I believe my sister Maria is slowly absorbing the Light and seeking the Truth.

I am grateful for the success of my work, and its continuing potential as it grows with the help of my colleagues. I am humbled to be of some help to young Bronx girls. I welcome the new doors that are being opened for me to spread my message of empowerment and spirituality to the young.

I am so grateful to God for bringing Peter into my life. His solid support is my rock to lean on, and with him I plan to build a beautiful home together. His commitment to our joint mission is a gift from Heaven. His attitude towards his parents has changed, and he now accepts them with love and appreciation.

I am grate ful to see how his parents have also changed by becoming less materialistic and more benevolent with their generosity. They have showed Peter and me with love and acceptance.

I am so blessed to have all these newly transformed people in my life, and I look forward to what awaits me in my future journey ahead.

Above all, I am so aware of my personal relationship with God, from whom I feel and receive a lot of love that enables me not only to love myself, but also to love others."

Gloria woke up the following day feeling happy. She stayed in her bed for a full twenty minutes before getting up, attentively creating her day with fresh positive thoughts. She realized she was inspired to learn how to meditate, and she realized Marco might be able to guide her on her initial choice of meditation.

On Saturday around six p.m., the Camino family gathered to go to Manhattan in two chauffeured cars to meet the other side of their new family.

All seven members of the Camino entourage, including Lula, Marco's fiancee, looked striking in their formal dresses and suits. They left the house in two cars at 6:30, and arrived at thirty-five minutes later in front of the Shepard's mansion in Manhattan.

Peter met them at the main door when the bell rang, and he was joined by his parents soon thereafter. Peter introduced the guests to his parents, who welcomed them to their home. After a minute or so of greetings, they all moved to the spacious living room to enjoy the drinks served by the butler and housekeeper.

They exchanged warm congratulations to the newly engaged couple, and Gloria then mentioned that Marco and Lula to be congratulated as well.

Joseph addressed Luca and Louisa, saying, "I want you to know that your are the parents of a unique and magnificent child, and we are honored to have Gloria as our new daughter. We love her dearly already, and we are proud to see her making a life with our son Peter."

Luca responded with, "We are honored to meet you and Monica. Gloria has told us much about you and your loving generosity that is going to enable her and Peter in their future undertakings together. We are with you in this regard, and Luisa and I are doing whatever we can as parents to help them in their future journey. Their presence in our lives has notably influenced and transformed the way we live too. My only son Marco is quite determined to help and to accompany his sister Gloria and his new brother Peter on their new spiritual and moral path."

After a while, the combined families took their seats at the long dining room table. The Shepard's chef had prepared a delicious three-course dinner. Joseph made sure it was served with an excellent Italian wine that he felt sure Luca and his family would like.

Around dessert time, Peter informed everyone that he and Gloria decided on their wedding day, and the affair would take place about forty days from now, in the month of June. They were all excited to hear this news, and everyone offered to help since the time to plan was short.

Peter told both sets of parents that he and Gloria had decided the choice of venue was up to them. Peter and Gloria then begged them not to do anything fancy, but their two fathers looked at them for a moment before Luca said, "Please allow us to enjoy hosting this unique event, since it is something that we all have been eagerly awaiting." Joseph and Luca then discussed the matter for a while, until they finally agreed to have the wedding ceremony at St. Thomas Church and the reception at the Waldorf-Astoria Hotel, pending availability, of course.

Hearing the plan, Gloria looked at Peter and whispered, "I told you so!"

Gloria then told the Shepherds about their vision.

"Peter and I have decided to open an education center at the building you donated to our organization. We plan to call it, "Shepherd Awareness Center," or SAC. We wish to offer a huge library of spiritual and self-help books and magazines on the first floor, with a lecture room and classrooms on the remaining floors.

"Peter and I will have our offices in the building, and we wish it to serve as our headquarters for all our joint activities and projects. So again, we thank you together one more time. And, while I am on the subject of generosity, I also would like to thank my parents and Marco for donating two more Mercy Centers to treat teenage girls in the Bronx. We are so blessed and grateful to have you as our parents."

Peter then seized the opportunity to tell everyone that Gloria was going to be a keynote speaker at three national conferences. "I am so proud of my future wife," he said, and everyone clapped.

The rest of the evening went very well, ending with hugs and kisses all around at 10:30 p.m.

After the Caminos departed, Joseph told his son, "Peter, if you are planning to work out of the Queens building, perhaps you and Gloria might be interested in living in an apartment I have vacant on the East Side of Manhattan, and situated close to the Queensboro Bridge leading to Queens. This will save you from experiencing much of the traffic frequently found throughout Manhattan. What do you think?"

"Dad, this is incredible! What a coincidence! Where is it located exactly?"

"It is on 62nd street and 1st Avenue, close to the Bridge on 59th street. The building has twenty-three floors, and the two-bedroom apartment is on the twelfth floor. If I recall, it has a nice view of the East River and Queens. It is about 2,000 square feet, and also offers a study. There is twenty-four-hour security, and concierge service. You are welcome to furnish it the way you please. The place, and its new furnishings, are on me as well. Consider all a wedding present!"

"This is amazing, dear father, and thank you so much. When can Gloria and I see it?"

"I asked for the keys yesterday when I found out it became vacant. Here you are; the apartment is yours," Joseph said, handing him the keys.

Peter then did something he rarely offered his father: He approached him and hugged him from all his heart. Monica observed their embrace with tears of joy pooling in her eyes. When Peter stepped back, he went over and thanked his mother as well with an affectionate hug and misty eyes.

The next day, Father John told Gloria that the third Center could open in two days, and all the newly hired staff was prepared and ready for the grand opening. He also told her that he never saw any article about her interview in *American Atheist* magazine.

Gloria requested, "Please invite some dignitaries to the opening of the third Center, and start welcoming new applicants. And how Emma is doing with the books, and how much money do we have available in the account?'"

"Emma is doing a great job with the books, and she tells me she is happy and satisfied in her relationship with Jared; the young man seems to have truly changed in his behavior and lifestyle. As for the organization's account, we have about $270,000 available, thanks to continued generous donations from new people.'"

Father John then gave Gloria the dates for the three conferences. She noted that the NYC and Pittsburgh ones would happen before her wedding day, while the Chicago conference was set for early July.

"May I consult with you on something personal if you have the time?'" Father John asked unexpectedly, interrupted Gloria's thoughts.

"Father, I am always available to you anytime. Go ahead.'"

"Diana and I are in love with one another. She and I have agreed that I should be the one to inform you, and ask for your blessing.'"

"That is great news! I appreciate you telling me, and of course I bless your relationship with each other. I hope you two decide to get married within a short amount of time! Congratulations, and I will come over tomorrow to see Diana in person and extend my good wishes. God, this is good news!'"

"Thank you so much, and God bless you too.'"

Right before Gloria went home after work, Peter called her to say he had some good news to tell her. She asked him to wait, and tell her when he joins her family for dinner at seven o'clock. Peter agreed.

At the Camino mansion, Gloria was able to enjoy a few private moments with her brother Marco before Peter arrived.

"Marco, I am so thrilled to hear of your engagement! Have yo and Lula have decided on a date for your big day?'"

"We are thinking sometime in September, before the weather gets cold. I plan to ask Peter to be my best man, and Lula has told me she would love to have you as her maid of honor, for you are like the sister she does not have.'"

"Hmm, what an honor for Peter! I also think Peter has you in mind for his best man; now how about that? I am honored that Lula is considering me, and I look forward to being in her wedding!

It is interesting that in the next few months, there will be three weddings: yours, mine and Diana's!'"

"Diana too?" Marco replied, visibly surprised. "To whom?'"

"Father John. They have become close working together at the Centers.'"

"You are kidding! I thought he is a priest!'"

"He used to be, but that what people know him by?

"Well, it is great news, and I am thinking we should all get a discount somehow!" Marco joked.

"Why don't you ask one of your spiritual mentors to officiate? They can marry us for free. I am sure our poor parents will be happy!" Diana grinned.

"Okay, I'll check if the Dalai Lama is available!" Marco chuckled.

Before brother and sister could continued their joking, Peter walked into the room. Gloria greeted him with a kiss on both cheeks and said, "Guess what? Marco said he can arrange for the Dalai Lama to marry us.'"

Peter stopped for a second, eyeballed her face and Marco's, then said, "I don't believe you—and you two should start taking life more seriously.'"

"Yes, boss!!!" Gloria and Marco said simultaneously before breaking out into laughter again.

"Marco, tell Peter whom you have chosen as your best man!" Gloria urged while still giggling.

"You, Peter!" Marco said.

"Really? Did Gloria tell you whom I have chosen?" Peter asked Marco as a grin of approval spread across his features.

"Well, me of course! Whom else would you trust to hold the rings?"

As the two men hugged and patted one another on the back. Luca walked out from his office.

"What is all this fuss about?" he asked, as it was obvious something was afoot.

Marco told him, and after Luca nodded his head in pleasure, Peter said, "I also have something to tell you all!"

Peter looked at Gloria, picked up her hand to hold and said, "Sweetheart, we have a home already!" He took the keys to the apartment out of his pocket, jiggled them and added, "My father gave me the keys to a vacant apartment he owns on the East Side!"

"You are kidding me! We have a home already?" Gloria shrieked enthusiastically. "Tell me more, darling!"

"It is on the twelfth floor of a modern twenty-three-floor high-rise building with a concierge and twenty-four-hour security. The apartment is about 2,000 square feet, and it has two large bedrooms and a study. My father tells me it offers great views of the East River and Queens. One of the best things about it is its perfect location: It is at 62nd and First, which is only two blocks away from the entrance to the Queensboro Bridge."

The young couple move close together and shared a joyous embrace as Luca and Marco congratulated them on the good news.

Marco immediately teased, "Yeah! I have a place to stay in Manhattan now."

"Make sure you call us before you come so we can alert the concierge! Otherwise, with the way you look, he's sure to keep you out of the building!" Gloria joked.

"Is the place furnished?" Marco asked Peter.

"No, it will be up to use to choose furnishings for the space, but my father said he will pay for these as part of our wedding present.

So, sweetheart, we had better get started looking for the furniture since we don't have a lot of time left."

Luca stepped into the conversation at this point.

"A friend of mine has a very nice modern furniture store here in the Bronx. I will ask to him to give you a good discount, and to arrange for a fast delivery once you've made your selections."

"That will help out. Thank you, Dad."

"I will go with you; I know the man, and I am familiar with his showroom. I'll choose my own bedroom set for your place there," Marco said with a grin.

"There's going to be no bed for you, dear brother. You can sleep on the floor if you insist on barging into my new place!"

They all laughed at Gloria's comment, and then the conversation shifted the conversation to the forthcoming marriage ceremony.

Gloria said, "I've already retained a wedding planner, and she is already busy working on dozens of details. Peter and I will get an update soon. Mom and Maria are accompanying me this weekend to help choose the dresses—and no, you are not invited, curious Marco! Peter and I have an appointment next week with the bishop and another priest in regards to the church ceremony. I am not sure if the reception hall has been booked already; do you know, Dad?"

"No, I don't. Joseph said he would take care of it. I will call him for you and find out.'"

"Thanks, Dad. Did the two of you discuss the number of guests that will be invited?"

"He and I started with about one thousand as the number, but we've settled for maximum of five hundred guests; is that okay?

"Seriously, Dad? Five hundred? Please trim it down to a max of two hundred and fifty, please.'"

"I'll see what I can do, but I will have to talk Joseph again. We are certain to offend many friends this way if we go with such a low number and they don't get an invite.'"

"Thank you, Dad, but I really don't want such a large number, and I already know Peter feels the same way.'"

Gloria darted a look at her fiance, and he gave a nod of agreement.

After enjoying a wonderful dinner, Gloria and Peter excused themselves and went to her office to work on Gloria's forthcoming speech at the national conference being held in New York. Gloria was determined to include in her message her new thoughts regarding the quality of life the young should consider. She told Peter that she did not want to be associated with the her current work at the Centers only, but to use that experience and background as a launching pad to greater things that involve the wellbeing of youth of both genders.

Peter took handwritten notes of her remarks as she mentioned her ideas aloud, and after two hours of her deliberation, he had filled eight pages on his yellow pad. He told Gloria he would work on fine-tuning the message later that night, and they will go through the speech the next day again.

They two agreed that her speech should end up being more or less the same in all three conferences, as Gloria wanted to drive her main message home to as large an audience as possible.

"Peter," Gloria wondered, "Do you think I can deliver the speech impromptu as I become familiar with it?'"

Peter answered "Yes, it is quite possible, especially if you memorize in advance the main points you wish to make. But you may want to have them written down on an index card, just in case. You're a smart lady, and you can deliver an amazing message without having to read it all, I believe!'"

❧ CHAPTER 15 ❧

Spirituality for All

⟨❧⟩

The first conference took place at the Grand Hyatt New York on Forty- Second Street. The lecture room had a capacity for an extremely large audience with its approximate 26,000 square foot size.

Gloria's speech was scheduled at 10:30 am on Monday, the second day of the conference. There were 1,400 participants comin from all over the United States and from sixteen other countries around the world. The theme of the conference was, "The Future of Our Youth.'"

The three-day conference had scheduled a total of twelve speakers tackling different subjects pertaining to the various life aspects of today's young people. Gloria was one of the three speakers on the spiritual aspect of the young.

Gloria waited to go out until she was introduced by the conference MC as, "*Gloria Camino, the Founder of four Mercy Centers and the youngest pioneer treating and teaching teenage girls to live a moral and spiritual lfe.*"

The sizable audience clapped when Gloria took the stage, and Gloria realized she was not at all intimidated by the sheer number of conference attendees.

She looked beautiful, dressed as she was in the same light blue pantsuit she wore at her own conference, and she also felt extremely confident.

Before starting her speech, Gloria looked around for a moment. She immediately spotted Peter and their two families seated in the middle of the conference room.

In a very relaxed manner, she started her impromptu speech. She held only one small card with a few handwritten reminders about the key points she wanted to make.

Gloria spent about seven minutes explaining the nature of her work and the inspiration behind establishing four Mercy Centers in the Bronx. She specified that the Centers treated about two hundred teenage girls total a year, and that half of the girls were pregnant and the other half suffering from severe emotional problems arising from violence and child abuse. She expressed gratitude for the Center's volunteers, the generous donations that kept pouring in, and the collaboration of nearby hospitals and clinics.

The second part of her speech went like this:

"I am very grateful for the accomplishments achieved thus far. The work we started will continue to expand in other parts of the city, the state, and hopefully the nation.

"Having said that, I am called by my Inner Voice, the Holy Spirit, to develop new programs and Centers that address the spiritual and moral needs of all young people, male and female!

"To start, my colleagues and I will soon be opening an 'Awareness Center' in Queens. The Center will be in a big building donated to us by a benevolent family present with us today.

"Our intention at this Awareness Center is to familiarize, teach and guide all young people, and their parents, how to conduct a more fulfilling spiritual life at home, and in school.

"We plan to have hundreds of spiritual books and articles available to hundreds of visitors through our library. Our goal is also to provide bi-weekly spiritual lectures by prominent spiritual leaders in our large auditorium that is currently under construction. Our regular programs will be oriented to teach spiritual lessons in ten different classrooms, all within the space of the same building. Why, you may ask?

"I believe that I am called by the Divine Power to help young people understand more easily the Love of God.

"This spiritual approach should appeal to people from all religions, as I am being called to preach the Universal Truth that we call Good" in the hope that this Truth be adopted and applied by everyone on an individual basis in their daily lives.

"I believe we all deserve to enjoy a personal relationship with our Creator and Supreme Soul. This relationship will bring more happiness and joy to our everyday life.

"A personal relationship with God takes us far beyond church buildings, synagogues, mosques or temples. We can remain as members of any of these religions and practice their teachings, but with a renewed radiant and vibrant soul that is aligned with the Source of all Energy.

"I believe that this new spiritual practice will enhance our own faith in the religions we grew up with.

"As for myself, I was born and raised as a Catholic Christian. The awareness I now have to forge a strong positive personal relationship with my Inner Being will not stop me for being a good Christian, but will further enhance my religious beliefs with greater appreciation and Joy.

"The awareness I am talking about applies to all people of all religions. It is a Universal Truth that is invisible and unseen, yet exists in each and every one of us. Once we are aware of its existence and we acknowledge its power, it helps us create our own reality.

"I pray that many adults will join me in my belief and create similar Centers in the communities in which they live across the nation and around the world, in order to help their own young people become further enlightened.

"I envision that we will achieve decreased violence and terrorism around the globe through establishing a foundation for world peace that will be led by the young people whom I describe here, as they are the leaders of tomorrow.

"I truly believe this blessed vision to be my mission for the remainder of my active life.

"Now I know why I was brought to this planet, and I know what the purpose of my life is.

"Thank you!"'

Gloria received a lengthy standing ovation. The audience clapped and roared, and offered up cheers and whistles. Gloria bowed her head three times in gratitude before she left the stage to go back to her seat.

During the lunch break, reporters, cameramen and other participants approached Gloria to get a closer look at her and ask probing questions. After several minutes of this, Gloria walked out with Peter and their families to enjoy lunch at a nearby restaurant.

As they dined, the families congratulated her on her impromptu speech and how charismatic she was on stage. Peter told her that the participants were fully focused on her words and the manner in which she expressed them.

"I swear to God, I saw a halo all around you when you were up there,'" Peter said with conviction.

After her first two national conference exposures in New York and Pittsburg, the word of Gloria as being an important and essential young spiritual pioneer spread fast across the nation. Invitations to speak at other events in future, and interview requests, kept pouring in.

Despite this active media attention, Gloria remained humble and focused on the task at hand. The three Mercy Centers were operational and occupied to full capacity, with the fourth Center almost ready to open. Gloria's wedding to Peter was fast approaching, followed a week later by the wedding of Father John and Diana. Meanwhile, the building plans for the Awareness Center were complete, with the only delay arising from awaiting the departure of the building's current occupants.

Peter started working on a new website called "Youth Awareness,'" which he planned to launched at the same time SAC is opened. He also established a new non-profit organization called 'Awareness Centers.' This organization was separate, in terms of mission, accounting and much of the staff, from the one established for the 'Mercy Centers.' Doing so allowed his father's gift of the building to be tax-deductible as a charitable donation.

The generosity of Peter's and Gloria's fathers did not cease: Joseph opened a living trust in the amount of $5 million in the name of Peter, while Luca established three trusts of $1.5 million for each one of his children as well. These trusts gave the beneficiaries the authority to use the money as they pleased. With that kind of money, Gloria and Peter had no concern whatsoever about their personal spending requirements.

Gloria felt so comfortable with the state of her finances that she gave Diana and Father John an early wedding gift of $20,000 from her newly enriched personal account. She told to put it towards a beautiful wedding and honeymoon. Gloria also told them to each take a week off for the honeymoon, and approved a 15 percent increase in their salaries starting the next month.

Diana asked Gloria to be her maid of honor, and Gloria's answer was, "I would be honored!" Father John asked his brother to be his best man.

Gloria decided on her sister Maria as her maid of honor, and Peter officially asked Marco to be his best man. Gloria chose a simple but beautiful white wedding dress for herself, and a light blue dress for her sister.

Wedding invitations were sent out to three hundred guests about three weeks in advance. Joseph confirmed that while the ballroom at the Waldorf- Astoria hotel had been booked for the reception, he also had reserved the hotel's presidential suite for the newlyweds to enjoy for three nights after the wedding.

As their wedding day approached, Peter and Gloria became a bit nervous, even though their love for one another had grown to even higher levels since their engagement two months earlier. Their faith in one another and in their future was complete. They had a gentle and deep respect for one another. The two truly did not care much about the lavish wedding arrangements their parents had, and they could not wait to be active again in the mission that awaited them after the big day.

The couple's wedding ceremony at St. Thomas Church started precisely on time. Gloria walked in holding her father's arm to the Wagner's Bridal March, and everyone stood. Father and daughter walked down the long, tastefully decorated aisle, to where Peter waited with a huge smile on his face.

Peter and Marco, who were on the left side, looked fantastic in their smart black tuxedos, while Maria, who was on the right side, looked ethereal in her blue dress. The Bishop and two other priests were standing behind them on the altar.

The wedding ceremony took about forty minutes before the Bishop said, "You may kiss the bride!" The newlyweds enjoyed their first long kiss announcing the end of their celibacy and the beginning of a new life together. The audience cheered the new Mr. and Mrs. Shepard on their way out of the church to the limousine that took them to the nearby hotel.

The reception at the hotel was extravagant and perfect. About two hundred and eight guests went to sit at their assigned tables. The party officially started at seven o'clock with the first dance of the bride and groom to the song they had chosen by Barry White, "You're my First, My Last, My Everything." Luca then danced with his daughter to the music of his favorite Italian singer, Zucchero, and the love song "Diamente."

The rest of the party then continued, with many dancing from time to time to the music of the band. After cocktails and some general chatter, a five- course seated dinner was served beginning at 8:30 p.m. It lasted for two hours.

Marco stood up to give a speech with a glass of champagne in his hand.

"Gloria, my little sister, you have become so big in my eyes, and you have filled my life with hope since you turned eighteen. I loved you when we were kids, but I respect you much more now as a mature spiritual teacher and humanitarian. Your love of God and humanity cannot be equaled, and I am proud to call myself your brother. When you go to live with your new husband, I will miss the daily frequency of our shared jokes and laughter. I will miss your radiant and vibrant presence at our parents' home.

"As for you, Peter, don't feel left out! I have come to respect you and love you as the brother I never had. Your commitment to love and to help Gloria is a great example for us all. Your humility and great manners offer great lessons from which we all should learn. I look forward to a long relationship with you full of friendship and brotherhood, and I am sure you will take wonderful care of my dear sister Gloria.

"I love you, and God bless you both!"

The guests started clinking glasses at the end of Marco's speech, and many began requesting Gloria to say something as well. She had expected this, and she stood up confidently with her own glass of champagne in her hand.

"Honored guests, family and friends, I am delighted that you found the time to join Peter and me today as we celebrate our love.

"I thank you, my dear sister and maid of honor, for your love and non- judgmental support. Maria, you will always be a good example, as a mother, a sister and a wife.

"I thank my in-laws for bringing Peter into the world. Without you, Monica and Joseph, we wouldn't be here today.

"Mom and Dad, you are the perfect couple who has endured all things with the strength of love! I have witnessed your understanding of one another, your dependability on one another, and above all, your unconditional love for one another and your children. You taught my siblings and me the value of being together through the good times, and also never to give up during the difficult times. I hope that what Peter and I have will be as special and powerful a relationship as yours has been, and continues to be.

"And to you, my dear brother Marco I am grateful for our developing spiritual bond that cements my admiration of you.

"And to you, my love, where do I start? I never thought I would be standing here today with your ring on my finger, and sharing your name. In you, Peter, I have my best friend and my life partner. Thank you for your love, your friendship and your support. Thank you for the joy you have brought into my life. I look forward to making our dreams a reality as we share this incredible journey together.

"To everyone, please enjoy the rest of the evening and join me in a toast ... to Love!'"

The entire room wildly applauded. In the midst of this applause, Peter stood up and kissed Gloria on her lips, which only added to the uproar in the room. Then he addressed the room again once the applause died down.

"I thank you all for participating in this divine union of our marriage. I cannot thank God enough for Gloria's acceptance to be my wife.

"Gloria, you are my shining star that guides me, the light that eliminates all darkness, the love that eradicates all fear, and the hope for an amazing future.

"Everybody loves you, not only for your stunning personality and magnetic character, but also for the endless ocean of love, compassion and generosity you extend to people you don't even know! I am honored to be your husband, and I will always be there for you and support you in the fulfillment of your calling. I love you for who you are.'"

The reception continued past midnight. However, the newlyweds discretely thanked and informed their parents they were sneaking out around midnight. They did so, rushing up to their suite with light giggles to celebrate their marriage privately and passionately for the first time.

Gloria and Peter Shephard spent three wonderful days together in their suite at the Waldorf. This was their only honeymoon, as they were eager to continue with their charitable works.

In those days together, they enjoyed the warmth and intimacy generated by the union of their bodies, and their discovery of the new physical pleasures of togetherness. They ate, slept and played in the rooms of their suite, and never left it until it was time to leave.

When it was time for them to check out of the hotel, both sets of parents met them at the hotel and accompanied them to their newly furnished apartment in the city.

As Peter carried Gloria over the threshold, the newlyweds knew this signaled a new chapter in their life as a couple, as well as a renewed dedication to an amazing future full of unknown experiences. Their mutual intentions were that these experiences be meaningful and beneficial to all people who crossed their paths.

Gloria's life purpose had been made clear—her mission was to enlighten to others—and already all her dreams were being fulfilled. all, that is, except for one more!

CHAPTER 16

Finding and Spreading the Message

During their three-day hotel honeymoon, Gloria and Peter had had ample time—apart from spending a lot of time in bed together, that is—to talk about their future plans and what to do about the 'unified message' on their minds for so long. So, on their second evening together as a married couple, and after having just enjoyed the true pleasures of physical love, they ordered up room service for dinner. Then, clad in the hotel's comfortable guest bathrobe, Gloria stretched out on the sofa with her head in Peter's lap as Peter opened up the subject again.

"Gloria my love, I have an idea regarding your search for a single message of love that might unite the world into following one all-encompassing spiritual path. Would you like to hear it?'"

"Of course, sweetheart! Please enlighten me.'"

"It is may sound crazy, but hear me out. I was reading an article last week about the benefit of artificial intelligence, or AI, in the field of physical health, and how it has accelerated the diagnosis and treatment of several illnesses. Physicians now have access to computer software learning programs through which a patient's illness can be diagnosed much more accurately and quickly. Such a diagnosis may take mere minutes, whereas before it may have takendays, weeks or months to figure out what was going on before.'"

"How is this related to my wish in the spiritual realm, Peter?" Gloria asked, completely confused.

"We now live at a time where computing power and the availability of online data has grown to extremely high levels! Huge companies with search engines like Google and Facebook have access to tremendous data banks and amazing computing algorithms that operate at very powerful speeds. They have developed highly sophisticated computer programs, referred to as 'Deep Learning programs,' where machines can see and recognize images, talk and interact with users in different languages, and the like. These programs teach computers how to think, and mimic the human brain in several capacities in ways that can end up outsmarting human intelligence.'"

"Interesting! It seems you are a bit of an expert in Artificial Intelligence now, my love! Please tell me what you have in mind for our humble life.'"

"My beloved wife, think of the huge amount of data that is available online regarding all the religions in the world, as well as the recent avalanche of spiritual books and teachings. It would take years of work for any human to try and sort out what essential teachings are common throughout these religions and spiritual thoughts. A person would need to study and decipher.. .a million pages or more to distinguish what would be relevant to this search for commonality

"However, if you program a Deep Learning program to do this kind of work, the selection process can be achieved in a matter of days, if not less!

"Programmers can write programs with a required goal as an 'Input,' which allow the machines with such programs to do the selection by searching the huge data at an astronomical speed until it comes out with the anticipated outcome, or 'Output.'"'

"Excuse my ignorance on this subject, Peter, but how do you know what to tell the machine to search for?'"

"I assume if you were to instruct a computer with this kind of learning program to look for any religious or spiritual reference on the subjects of Love, Happiness and Peace, it will do the job we desire. There must then be some capacity in the program that would allow for further editing or shortening of the amount of material it finds on theses subjects. You should be able to ask the search program to simply continue on, filtering out the relevant information as required by the person inputting the request.'"

"What if the end result comes out with hundreds or thousands of pages, sweetheart? This would not be the simple and direct message I have in mind!'"

"Yes, it is possible that would be the result, my dear, and if that happens, we would need to consult with an expert in the field as to whether if the material can be abridged into a smaller collection of essential pages by the machine itself. I don't know all the answers; I brought up the matter just to impress upon you the possibility that it can be done. What do you think of the possibility?"

"The process makes sense," Gloria allowed, "as long as the end message is humanly edited, and not artificially produced. Let us work on developing this idea further. We can continue discussing it through seeking guidance and opinions from other trusted sources. Peter, I am impressed how smart you have become since our wedding," Gloria teased. "Marriage suits you!'"

A week later, they had dinner at the Shephard's mansion in Manhattan, and Peter shared the idea of using AI learning machines to develop a program that would bring about a written message of Love, Peace and Happiness derived from all traditional religious books and current spiritual writings.

Joseph's eyes lit up at this news, and he immediately articulated that he had a friend who was an AI expert, and who might be able to shed further light on the idea. He promised to set up an appointment for Peter and Gloria to meet with him.

"However," Joseph pointed out, "even if my friend can advise you on the technical part of this project, I believe the real problem lies in the attitude of the religious leaders who may eventually stop any such declaration of a new teaching.'"

"What do you mean, Dad?'"

"Well, you cannot assume that the leadership of Christianity, Islam and Judaism, who are all powerful guardians of the three monolithic religions that believe in One God, would agree to any modification of their traditional doctrines. Peter, you know your professors at the Seminary; why don't you consult with them first on what such a reaction from the leadership might be?'"

"I will do that, Father, and see what they say.'"

Peter went to the Seminary with Gloria the next day and asked to meet with Father Matthew, a highly regarded professor and the head of Religious Studies at the Seminary. They met with him in his office and explained what they had in mind. The Father started fidgeting in his chair after about ten minutes of listening to Gloria and Peter. He then said, "I admire your attempt to build a.. .a 'triangular bridge' of spiritual commonality between the three religions. However, I do not believe you will succeed in introducing a doctrine in common that would be accepted by any of the three of them. You may not realize you are tackling something of a political issue here!

"Each religion's leaders will hold dearly onto the teachings in their holy books, be it the Bible, the Quran or the Torah. Many prior attempts have been made by scholars to establish cross-references between the three holy books, but none of these attempts have succeeded in bringing about any change in terms of a particular religious tradition modifying its original writings. You are free to express your ideas of course, and while those ideas may appeal to certain individuals from these religions, you should not expect the religious leadership to go along with such thoughts and recommendations.'"

Gloria said, "Father, the intent is not to persuade members of these religions to *abandon* their traditional faiths and beliefs, but to introduce them to a more universal understanding of spirituality, one that is still based upon a personal relationship between them and God."

Father Mathew leaned closer to his desk and said in a firm tone, "Then just write a book expressing your opinion in this regard, and leave it to the individuals within each religious tradition to decide. But Ithat are based on attempts that have amission as y And know that religious leaders do not like change, nor any attempt to take away their power. Of course you are entitled to express your opinion—joining the ranks as you do so—but you cannot officially declare and advise people to follow a New Path. That would create a political war among the three religious leaders, who will reject any idea that may compromise their own teachings."

Peter stepped in and said, "Do you feel, Father, that we would be introducing something viewed as a.. .rebellious act against any or all of these three religions in requesting people to become more aware of what true spirituality is all about, even if we are not declaring a new doctrine? "

"In a sense, yes. Those who have tried such a thing before have brought about divisions, and created new sects, within their own religions. For example, you both know much about the history of Christian churches and its main divisions into Protestants, Catholics and Orthodox, and the dozens of subdivisions that mushroomed thereafter. Similarly, in Islam you have the divisions of Sunnis and Shiites, and their offspring sects. Judaism is not lacking either in its different schools of practice. Throughout history there have always been new attempts to reform or improve on what existed already. What has this led to, other than more divided religions and chaos?!"

"But that is exactly what we are trying to *change*, Father." Gloria emphasized.

"Our intent is to *unify*, not to divide."

With a serious face Father Matthew said in an emphatic voice, "Yes, my dear, but despite your good intentions, you cannot swim against the current. The religious powers-that-be will fight back and shut you down! It is unfortunate, but the traditional leadership does not allow anyone to infringe on their power to control their religions. You can start your own church, if you wish, but not declare war against these powers.

"Now, I understand from Peter that you are starting a Spiritual Awareness Center, and that is good. I understand its mission, and you can have as many of these as you want; it is a free country. You also can write as many books as you want, and you can hold as many seminars and conferences as you want. But I tell you, you will not succeed if you try to announce a new 'common' religion that combines the three main religions together under one umbrella."

Gloria stared at the ceiling for few seconds after hearing these words before she said, "We appreciate what you have said, Father Matthew, and we realize it would be a very hard climb up the hill. So Peter and I will ponder your remarks, and then we will abide by whatever divine guidance we may receive before we proceed with our plans."

The young couple thanked Father Mathew for his time and advice before leaving to discuss the matter further over some coffee at a nearby shop they knew.

"So, what do you think?" Peter questioned Gloria. "Or, how do you feel about what we just heard?"

"I don't know yet, Peter. I am somewhat confused.or maybe the truth is, I am disturbed by the.the power of these religious leaders. I still believe that we have to bring a new level of awareness to all people of different faiths. I do realize that the three monolithic religions are extremely hard-headed and powerful, so perhaps it would be easier to line up with Eastern religions who are more open-minded?'"

"Yes, I do agree that it would be, Gloria," Peter said with a nod of his head. "As a matter of fact, the new spiritual thoughts in the West got their inspirations from the East. But that is not what *our* challenge is! Our challenge is the other three religions that we talked about with Father Matthew."'

"Yes, of course you're right, and we should not get distracted from that. So we need to explore finding out the commonalities between these three religions via that AI research or program you raised. The resulting information or outcome will enlighten us further on what needs to be done.

"Now, if it turns out that we can only write books and open more awareness centers and give speeches around the world to send the message across, let it be! We will leave the rest to the Universe to decide."'

"That is a great attitude, my dear Gloria. We can only teach and spread the message, as Jesus did. He did not start the religion; his followers did. We will meet with the AI expert, get the research done as quickly as we can, then proceed with what we will be guided to do. I will call my father and see if he has gotten us an appointment with his expert."'

"Sounds good. I need to visit with the Mercy Centers now while you go check on the construction work for the education center in Queens."'

Gloria was happy to learn that all four Mercy Centers were running smoothly, and that Father John had been doing a marvelous job in managing them. She had one more national conference to go to in Chicago in two weeks. She decided to take few more days off to spend vacation time with Peter, who would be joining her there.

When Peter called his dad to inquire at the AI expert, Joseph told his son that the man, Dr. Jonathan Brandon, would meet them in his office in on Thursday afternoon.

When Thursday arrived, Peter and Gloria went to the meeting, and met the well-known AI expert, who was working as a consultant to many firms keen to incorporate AI systems in their companies. Peter explained the job required, and the reasons behind it, to which Dr. Brandon replied,

"I see. This is a definite first. Fortunately, the task is technically simple and can be done as a narrow, not general, AI system." With a smile on his face, he added, "The friction that has existed for a long time between science and religion seems to be diminishing nowadays. There are several quantum scientists who are embracing a spiritual approach to their studies, although I must say, your project is a unique and different one.

"The data exists, and the algorithm can be developed. I need to ask a major search engine company if they can find time to do it. They are all moving at a mind-boggling pace in order to be ahead of the rest of the companies in developing more sophisticated Deep Learning machines.'"

"It is good to hear, Dr. Brandon, that the desired information can be obtained in the manner Peter had described to you. How long would such a project take, and how costly will it be?" Gloria inquired.

"Once a time slot is allocated by the developers for such a task, it should not take more than a week to program the machines with the necessary inputs and put together the matching algorithms. Thereafter, and due to the tremendous computing power that is now available, it takes only a matter of few days for the programs to sift through the huge amount of data and bring about the desired output.

"It is important to bear in mind though that such a literary-filtering has not been done before, so I will need to make some further inquiries with my friends and get back to you on the cost; I have no idea what this will be. What I can tell you is that data has become a very expensive commodity nowadays. I will call you back on the matter as soon as I can.'"

Gloria re-iterated her commitment to her message at any cost. She told Peter that the information outcome that such 'magical' machines would spit out was priceless, and it would be extremely original.

Peter remained silent, for he understood her zeal to reach out and bring a message to the global masses. However, he was quite concerned about their ability to surpass the power of the three religions however.

Gloria is the visionary, and I am the realist, he thought to himself.

Gloria and Peter went to dine with Gloria's parents at the Camino mansion that day. Marco was present, and he listened intently to their intriguing idea about using AI machines to help obtain the information they desired. Marco responded, "What an amazing idea!" Marco said with great enthusiasm. "I have also heard about how fast this AI technology is growing. Imagine the amount of time one would save with your task, compared to a job done manually! I hope you will succeed in doing it, and also that you can afford it. I have heard this kind of work is not cheap.'"

"No problem, dear brother; if it is very expensive and we can't fully fund it, I know we can count on your trust money as well," Gloria said with a smile on her face.

Luca was listening, and he looked at both, eyebrows raised and face growing a bit pale. He feared that the two of them might spend all their money he had just given them on something he did not quite understand, and could only refer to as 'this AI thing.'

"I am just joking, Dad!" Gloria said, soothing her father's nerves. "We don't know how much it will cost yet, but if it is beyond our budget, Peter and I may ask you and the Shephards for some additional funding.'"

Peter then explained slowly and quietly to Luca what it is that AI Deep Learning machines do.

When Luca finally understood the nature of their discussion and the technology assist behind it, he told them he would be willing to help if need be.

Gloria again teased her dad by saying, "Father, do not worry! We will just will use Marco's money instead if it turns out to be too rich for our blood!'"

Everyone at the table had a good laugh, and the newlyweds left to go back to their new home in the city feeling quite good about the future manifestation of their idea.

Dr. Brandon called Peter the following Monday, and asked for a meeting that same afternoon. Both Gloria and Peter attended.

Dr. Brandon said, "There are two sets of good news here! The first good news is that the job can be done by a major company starting in twenty days. They need ten more days to finish the input programing along with the right algorithm.

"The other piece of good news is that they are prepared to do the job for free if the order to do the work is done by a non-profit organization, and if they can keep their reserved rights to the final outcome. If you agree. here the relevant documents to sign, including the property title agreement.'"

Gloria questioned, "Excuse my ignorance in these matters, Dr. Brandon, but are you saying that the final outcome, which will be the basis of our message, will not belong to us?'"

"Let me clarify, Mrs. Shepherd. The actual work of collecting data and selecting the necessary or relevant information you seek is a software program, which is referred to as 'intellectual property.' That program will always be the property of the developer. You, as the organization that requested the work, will get the right to use the outcome to write your own message. In other words, you get the right to compose your own message based on the findings, but they keep the right to the program that was used to allow you to write your message.'"

"Does that mean that other groups or individuals could have access to the same program, and do with it what they like in the future?'"

"Legally, the developer has the right to share or sell the information to whomever they please. However, the agreement I have here stipulates that you will have the exclusive right to use the data exclusively for three years.'"

There was a moment of silence before Peter asked, "Why are they willing to do this work for free, Dr. Brandon?'"

"Partly because it is tax-deductible, and partly because they will own the intellectual property rights to something that is quite unique, something that is being done for the first time. The estimated cost, as per this document, is $850,000, which will become a deductible expense to their corporation. This cost could be recuperated by them, at a later stage, from others due to the program's great value.'"

Peter and Gloria looked at one another and without words knew what the other was thinking. So Peter told Dr. Brandon that they agreed to the terms.

Gloria and Peter signed and initialed the relevant documents that would allow the company to proceed with the task. They thanked Dr. Brandon for his mediation, and for waiving any fee for his efforts. He had helped them purely out of his great respect for his friend Joseph, Peter's father.

On the way home, Gloria expressed her deepest gratitude to God, who had guided them to this intuitive task. The two eagerly started visualizing the anticipated message in their head, and could not wait to see the end result within short.

After four years behind bars during which he had been following the news of, and media attention give to, Gloria's charitable work, Andrea had changed. So he wrote letters from prison asking for forgiveness from his own father, and from Gloria in particular.

Gloria beseeched her father to request his release on probation, and Luca finally agreed to ask his lawyers to work on the case. Gloria's request was an act that revealed her courage, forgiveness and compassion.

Three months later, Andrea's case was re-opened in court. Both Luca and Luciano were in the courtroom when the judge ordered the release of Andrea under probation and close supervision by the police. When Andrea spied his and Gloria's father hug in a friendly manner, he came over to shake Luca's hand in thanks and remorse, then give his father a big hug asking for his forgiveness.

When Gloria heard the news of Andrea's release, she asked to see him. Father John, who by now was happily married to Diana, arranged for the meeting to be held at the first Mercy Center. He asked Andrea to come by the following day.

Father John escorted Andrea into her office. Gloria looked up to see Andrea looking a bit shaken and sporting a wan complexion. She immediately stood up, greeted him and gave him a brotherly hug. He broke out crying like a child, and begging for forgiveness.

Gloria asked him to relax and to take a seat. She also gave a minute to calm down.

When she looked at him after the time had passed, she saw a different person a man who looked more mature. She noticed he was well built, elegantly dressed and sporting a short haircut.

Gloria put on a serious face as she said, "Well, Andrea, it has been several years since I saw you last. I want you to know that I forgive you for the mistakes you made, for we are not all perfect. I hope you developed some skills while in jail, or learned something beneficial to your wellbeing. You are still young, and I am sure a big future awaits you.

"You may have heard about what I am doing now. You should also know that I am married to a great man, whose photo is right here. So let's agree to put the past behind us, and please let me encourage you to move on and live a happy life.'"

"Thank you, Gloria, for your kind words and for asking to see me. I was a misguided fool to treat you so badly and let my stupid and pride ego rule my cruel actions. I have to apologize sincerely one more time, and thank you so much for your forgiveness.

"I am fully aware of your lifetime achievements thus far from what I saw on TV and the speeches I heard you gave; I found them online, and I read them time and time again. I hold you in great esteem, and I congratulate you for your work to help the young and the needy. I am ready to serve you in any way you see fit. I want to follow in your footsteps and counsel the young also.'"

"I appreciate that, Andrea, and I will see what needs to be done in the Centers. Consider me your sister now. It was great seeing you again, and please give my regards to your father. I am very grateful to him for all his help and generosity.'"

That evening, Gloria's family expressed astonishment that Gloria had seen Andrea, and all admired her for her courage, ability to forgive and compassion. Marco offered to teach and hire Andrea as a real estate broker, while Peter said he could use him at the Center. They agreed to let Andrea choose, and he chose the latter.

The next day, Gloria worked as usual, then for a time close thed door to her office simply to reflect on how her life had evolved over the past four years.

She had enjoyed her time in NYU, at the convent, and at the Seminary.

She was grateful to be guided into establishing the Mercy Centers, to have met and married Peter, for her brother's spiritual growth, and for her gift of public speaking that was leading to empowerment of the young.

All in all, Gloria felt happy and content. She knew that the future would be full of new surprises, happy moments and great achievements.

She also knew that all is duetto the Divine Power of Love.

EPILOGUE

Seven hundred people showed up for the grand opening of the Shepherd Awareness Center in Queens. Peter honored his father Joseph by asking him to cut the ribbons on opening day. He also appointed him as chairman of the organization's board.

SAC's library already housed more than two hundred books, dozens of magazines, and a hundred videos and movies, all on spirituality. The materials had been selected with the main intention of attracting the attention of the younger generation.

The library room had four long tables and comfortable chairs for visitors to use while browsing the material in the presence of a librarian ready to help them in any way possible, whether it was finding more material on a particular topic, or understanding the content being viewed. The attending librarian allowed books to be checked out for a maximum of one week at a time.

Within six months SAC had received more than 3,000 visitors, and offered daily classes every week free of charge. Spiritual teachers and volunteers were on hand to teach and give scheduled lectures.

Approximately 1,200 young people registered to take out books and return them within a week. SAC also showed spiritual movies and documentaries every night for free.

Peter was in charge of running SAC's Education Center, while Gloria supervised the activities and growth of the four Mercy Centers. In the same sixmonth period, Gloria appeared on five national TV programs and gave six interviews to national newspapers. Her website was crowded with blog chats and questions from the site's visitors.

The four Mercy Centers were fully occupied 90 percent of the time. Father John continued to be a great manager, assisted by well-trained volunteers and staff. Donations continued to pour in from the community and other benevolent funds or individuals. The model of Mercy Centers that Gloria had started was copied and being used in nine other states on the East Coast.

Gloria was satisfied with establishing and running the four Mercy Centers, so she was thrilled to learn others were starting similar Centers in different areas and states.

During her evenings at home with Peter, Gloria spent much of the time writing a book that addressed the spiritual needs of the young. She was already recognized as a celebrity among many youth organizations and clubs around the nation, and had tens of thousands of fans, judging from the email and text messages she kept receiving.

Her first book, titled *Young and Powerful*, was published eleven months after her marriage, and became a bestseller on *The New York Times'* Inspirational list for several weeks.

Before the end of three years, Gloria went on to publish two more books elaborating on the same message. Her advice and vision was to invigorate young people to become more spiritual on an individual level, and to radiate their renewed energies to the same churches and communities with which they were connected.

By now many spiritual organizations recognized Gloria as the youngest and most influential non-denominational spiritual leader in the nation. Her teachings and opinions appealed to people of all religions. She even received the 'Book of the Year' award from a top spiritual publishing organization.

As for Marco and Lula, they were enjoying a very happy life together, and had two children in the three-year period after their marriage. Marco was a Director on the board of the Awareness Center, and his friendship with Peter had become very strong and meaningful. He showed up frequently at SAC to give lectures about modern spirituality and the Law of Attraction. Many young people enjoyed his speeches, and afterwards immersed themselves in reading the relevant material available to them in the SAC library.

Gloria's relationship with Peter was growing harmoniously, and while the two of them each had very busy schedules, they relished spending time together in the evenings and on weekends.

Two years after the opening of the first Awareness Center in Queens, Peter decided to use part of the money in his trust to open a second Awareness Center, this time in downtown Manhattan. His father helped him out with the funding. The new Center was slightly smaller than the first one, but quite active, abuzz with visitors from New York as well as foreigners from other states and countries.

Peter remained a solid rock of support to Gloria's visionary mission, and his contribution to her visionary work was unprecedented. Together they were working on the findings of the AI machine that had sorted out and summarized what is common from hundreds of thousands of pages from the teachings of the three main religions and the more recent spiritual teachings.

The machine-produced summary had turned out to be an astonishing two-hundred pages full of quotations and references from each of the three religions, and other related spiritual materials. So Gloria and Peter had agreed to take their time developing their thoughts and words for the intended message.

Peter spearheaded the work in deciphering the long summary and preparing a shorter edited version of the intended message that Gloria had in mind. They had three years of exclusive rights, which allowed them not to rush their work.

After a year of thorough deliberation and discussion of the material at hand, Gloria and Peter finally decided to modify their stance. They agreed not to produce a document that would encourage the adoption of a new spiritual path. They did not want to antagonize and offend the leadership of the three religions, who might, in turn, disrupt their thriving work. Gloria said she preferred to simply use the rich material that had resulted in the books she wrote and the speeches she gave. The 'findings' had cemented her own unifying arguments, and re-enforced her quest for increased spirituality and morality.

Gloria's mission expanded nationally year after year. She remained humble, and her shining light illuminated the hearts and souls of hundreds of thousands of people worldwide. She expressed her desire to merge traditional religious doctrines with new spirituality in her writings and speeches in a manner that did not offend the traditional religious leadership. She was peacefully aligned with her Inner Being and always aware of her purpose: to Serve.

Gloria touched the lives of many followers with her messages of Love, Joy and Peace.

Always, always, her motto remained:

Love Is All There Is.'

www.ingramcontent.com/pod-product-compliance
Lightning Source LLC
Chambersburg PA
CBHW021630120626
46545CB00002B/473